THE LETTER I
NEVER SENT

THE LETTER I NEVER SENT

A Memoir of Resilience

R. JEROME THOMAS

EMPRESS

EMPRESS
PUBLICATIONS
WWW.EMPRESSPUBLICATIONS.COM

I dedicate this memoir to my wife, Susan, who has supported me through this journey. She has encouraged me immensely by listening and giving me honest feedback. I have edited and rewritten several scenes because of her honest critique. That is the beauty of writing and personal development. Every word we write is a peeling away of another layer of our soul. But the peeling opens us to a greater ability to love others, love the Divine and love ourselves.

I want to thank my daughters who continue to inspire reflection and unconditional love. Though we may not communicate like before, I have peace knowing they are living full lives, and one day this memoir may serve as reference and inspiration into their story. To my siblings: Ronita, who has written her own memoir, *Coming to Forgiveness: A Daughter's Story of Race, Rage and Religion*, and Kelesha, who has expressed life's mystery and beauty through several musical compositions and CDs. I am humbled to add another piece to the Thomas children collection.

No book is written in a vacuum. I have been guided by a supportive community that began with the National Association of Memoir Writers who helped me with foundational chapters in 2016. Their weekly lessons and webinars taught me how to excavate my memories. The productivity from that work let me know I could not leave my discoveries in a box. Further along, I found another memoir process called 100 Day Book. This program gave me understanding about structure, conflict, dialogue, and voice. The pressure to write and submit material on time gave me a strategy to develop my writing style.

Finally, I discovered *Your Story Matters* by Leslie Leyland Fields. Her teaching and the feedback from the Mighty Networks community let me know my story had meaning, purpose, and significance. Their feedback has helped to crystalize the scene development and clarity in this memoir.

I am thankful for the ministry I have had for the past forty-plus years. In the words of John Steinbeck, "You can only understand people if you feel them in yourself." In my life, no one is a stranger to my heart. COVID-19 and retirement let me know that my story must be told. I pray you receive just what you need to brighten your day, and keep you spiraling up with hope and resilience.

In Memoria
Rev. Dr. R. Colby Thomas
Father Extraordinaire

All the people who impacted my life who caused me to sit down, ponder, reflect, and prayerfully assess my impact upon their lives.

Table of Contents

Foreword

This book by Robert Thomas is an exciting story of the moving power of God's miracles today with the people we know. This well-told story is detailed with breathtaking and awe-inspiring events that share valley and mountain peak stories of Robert J. Thomas, which should be made into a movie.

Since the parents of the Reverend Thomas left a rich legacy on my life and the lives of my children as well as the Bay Area in education, religion, and city government, you would assume that he climbed up their ladder of success. This book will open your eyes to see how difficult it is for children of privileged parents to be productive and positive in the eyes of the critical public. By the grace and mercy of the living God, my former student shares with us his inspiring story of the wonder-working power of God who helped him to find himself, his purpose for living, and for honoring his Creator.

I am honored to write the preface for this well-written book. Please enjoy it.

J. Alfred Smith Sr.
Emeritus pastor, Allen Temple, Oakland, CA
Emeritus professor, Berkeley School of Theology,
Berkeley, CA

Preface

The Letter I Never Sent is a narrative that delves into the depths of low self-esteem, lack of parental acceptance, personal deficiencies, and struggle. This is a story of resilience, where nobody gave the protagonist a chance.

From the first time I opened up the sacred text at four years old, I felt God was writing directly to me. The connection was so intimate, I kept a small testament in my pocket over my heart. Over time, the power of the Word permeated my decisions, drawing me closer to God with every encounter. The offering in this memoir is a small portion of the stories that enriched my life. I hope you receive encouragement from my journey. This is a story of triumph through it all.

There was a time in our society when a letter was the major form of communication. Individuals would wait months for a letter that would often change the course of their life. This is what happened to me. I have written several letters that were never sent, and each changed the trajectory of my life. I believe society has lost the ability to write letters, and the absence of these messages has affected the depth of relationships. I hope this memoir will create a revival in letter writing in the family, schools, and globally.

My passion for letter writing began when I started teaching at my first high school, in Machakos, Kenya. My desire to write letters started with my vow to pen three aerograms per day. Like a soldier on the front lines, I was motivated to tell the African experience. From walks to the watering hole, to heating up water for hygiene and eating purposes, to reading by candlelight, and watching out for fire ants, each step was eventful. My life was filled with the most primitive existence imaginable.

That same passion to listen to the narratives of others continued as I listened to parishioners, inmates, soldiers, and patients. Each story humbled and enriched my desire about the power of story.

I hope my story will encourage you to write your story. When we share our story, we realize that we are more alike than we are different. Telling our story may be the most unifying action of unconditional love. With love and resilience, we can heal the world!

Chapter One

A Fall Into Grace

"A man's heart plans his way, but the Lord directs his steps."
Proverbs 16:9

April Fools' Day, 1981. Three weeks had passed since Dad's death, and I was still in a stupor. For some reason, I couldn't shake the fact that Dad was gone. His physical absence affected everything; even simple tasks became complicated because my racing mind could not stay in the moment. I bumped my head several times, trying to escape the lowered entrance of my emotional dungeon. Though the sun was shining through the trees, my heart was filled with dark cumulus clouds.

I held a paintbrush in my right hand, attempting to do my Friday chores. Today's task was painting the second floor and balcony of the home where I rented a room. Eight months earlier, I had taken a room only three miles from school. On-campus housing was full, so this quaint spot in the Redwoods was the closest and best option.

Once a week, I paid in-kind rent on my detached basement by doing menial work for the 70-year-old widow who owned the house. The widow, Ms. Smith, was away running errands, and I was left alone painting the wooden floor of her master bedroom. As I held the can of sky-blue paint covering the floor with wild flourishes, the paint fumes hindered my concentration. Instead of starting at the opposite wall and working toward the door, I had inadvertently painted myself into a corner, all the way out to the balcony.

"How stupid!" I murmured to myself, "I really didn't think this task through." I took a long breath to recalibrate. How was I going to get down? I put the can down with the brush beside it and looked westward over the pine trees toward Mount Tamalpais. Looking at it, I thought how fortunate I was to live this close to a mountain again. I sensed there was some mysterious connection between me and the mountains. With a sigh, I gazed down in my reverie to the creek below as I leaned on the balcony rail, twenty feet above the ground.

"Oh no!" Suddenly, the rail broke, and I headed straight down to the cobblestones below. My life flashed before my eyes. Time slowed into nanoseconds. As I fell, my mind instantly returned to my father's funeral, the flashbacks vividly making their way back to my mind.

I could see myself sitting in the front row. Though I wanted to shed a tear, it was almost impossible to grieve. The worst possible thing had happened. Disaster had struck, and I had no plan B. I wondered, "What's next for me?" as I waited to be called up to the pulpit for sibling remarks.

"How did it come to this? Reverend Doctor Robert Colby Thomas, dead at 58? Are all the men in my family cursed? Uncle Bud died at 56 of throat cancer, and now Dad, also in his fifties, deceased from brain cancer. Can the men in my family handle stress? Am I doomed to an early demise?"

I could see the packed church, although my focus was on only two people: one deceased and the other sitting in the pulpit. Dad was dead, killed by his efforts to serve a church that wasn't always pastor-friendly. The members appeared to be sheep, but they were stubborn as donkeys and opinionated as crows.

The interim pastor, Rev. Snell, was alive but spiritually dead. Dad was obviously anointed with many gifts and talents.

I wondered what gifts he saw in this barber-turned-preacher. "Why make him his successor?" His interim assignment was frustrating, and this wasn't in the plan. "Where is the God of mercy and restoration?" I believed God had a unique plan, but I couldn't see it.

"God must have had a plan" when Bishop Amos rescinded my Dad's appointment, after two years, as the pastor of the premier Christian Methodist Episcopal (CME) church of Northern California in 1965. As a result, "God must have had a plan" for Dad to co-found Church of All Faiths (COAF). This stiff-necked church had caused his death.

Descending half of my conscious mind was trying to figure out how to break the intensity of this impact.

As my mind saw myself giving accolades to Dad, I took my seat as the audience applauded. I wished this applause could have been put on hold for forty years. As I leaned back in these pin-cushioned church pews, I waited for the heavens to open and give me a sign. The only voice I heard from God was, "Wait, I will make it plain for you by and by."

I put my forearms over my face to protect the shock to my head. I knew everything I had devised in my heart was going to change. As I prepared to hit the ground, I realized this fall "might be God's sovereign plan."

Chapter Two

Humble Thyself

"Search me, O God, and know my heart; try me, and know my anxieties; And see if there is any wicked way in me, and lead me in the way everlasting."
Psalm 139: 23-24

"Am I in heaven or hell?" My visual world went dark, and every sensation became numb. I mused, "Is this what death feels like?" The fall from twenty feet had knocked every vibrant impulse from my mind, heart, and soul. It was April Fools' Day, but this scenario was no joke. I lay motionless, considering how to assess this brokenness one movement at a time.

"Opened eyes, left eye blurry; right eye, clear; and the cobblestones looked red like they were supposed to. Neck aligned; right hand, present; left hand, attached but no feeling; hips, movement on the right, vibration on the left; feet—never realized how many bones were down there—right foot moveable, left foot, shaky. Think I'll just rest here a few minutes and do another scan one more time."

After the third scan, I lifted my upper body to a plank position to see if I could stand the pain. I brought my right leg to a forty-five-degree angle, leaning on my sore right knee. Propping myself, I faintly saw Ms. Smith drive up. She didn't speak, but her eyes followed me as I meandered down the driveway. Every bone felt out of alignment. I stooped from pain, looking, without a doubt, like the Hunchback of Notre Dame. I hobbled down the pathway, bending forward like a hobbit ducking into my hole.

Approaching the bedroom door, I tasted blood. The reflection in the mirror confirmed my worst thoughts—my head was bleeding. I was a mess; my face was unrecognizable, my Afro was disheveled, my clothes were torn, and my buttons were missing. Exiting my meager confines, the Ross City fire truck waited in the driveway to escort me to the local hospital four miles away. Ms. Smith must have called them. I felt like a dignitary riding in the passenger seat, with open air and no roof on this antique vehicle, driving eastward down Sir Francis Drake Boulevard. I had traveled this path for the past six months, five nights a week, cleaning doctor's offices for minimum wage.

The ER nurse cleaned bruises from my left hand and head and took a CT scan of both and an MRI of my right leg to complete the preliminary assessment. I was broken, humbled, and embarrassed. The X-rays showed a long gash on the right side around my prefrontal cortex, needing twelve stitches. Radiology revealed a broken left wrist and slightly torn ligaments on my right knee. The ER staff sized a set of crutches for my six-foot frame, put gauze on my stitches, placed my left arm in a sling, and wrapped my right leg with an Ace bandage. It was nearing dark when the fire truck returned to my dungeon, and I crawled into bed and stayed there.

This inadvertent accident was a humbling experience. I was on the precipice of my largest social justice endeavor. For twenty years, since my dad had worked with Martin Luther King, Jr. in Mississippi, I had wanted to be involved in the movement for social change. For four months, community organizer Denise Gums and I had been planning a "Save the Children" protest intended to bring attention to the twenty-eight children killed in Atlanta since 1979. This event, scheduled for April 2nd in Oakland, was supposed to be my first venture into a leadership role and a social justice initiation. After this protest, I was confident the community would undeniably know that "I was down for the cause."

I called Denise and told her the news of my fall. She suggested that I rest, but I was determined to participate. The following day, I hobbled to my petite Honda Civic, sandwiched myself into the driver's seat, and showed up like a patched Humpty Dumpty at the protest site. Denise had arranged a wheelchair as I propped my right leg at ninety degrees, and she pushed me as the group marched behind us down Broadway toward City Hall.

Though my body was mangled, it didn't hinder my spirit from engaging in the call-and-response chant, "I won't let nobody turn me around, turn me around, turn me around, ain't going to let nobody turn me around, going to keep on walking, keep on talking, walking down freedom land." The turnout of the community—at least 500 people—let me know we had accomplished our mission. Showing up at that event taught me resilience and compassion. I continued to fight for the outraged people and their children until the perpetrator was apprehended.

Sunday morning, Ms. Smith knocked on my front door, wanting to talk. "Because you can't fulfill your weekly house obligation," she said, "you're going to have to move." I sulked momentarily, but my gut said, "The time has come to move on."

So, in April 1981, God's divine plan unfolded. This season of a ministry that I did not want to pursue unrolled like a prophetic scroll. Spiritually, I felt like Jonah, the reluctant prophet. Nothing in my natural abilities had prepared me for ministry. But unbeknownst to me, before I was born, plans were set in place for this work. While I was being formed in my mother's womb, divine plans were being formulated—congregants from the church where my dad had served as pulpit supply had been praying. Months after my dad's ordination as a CME pastor, another household of faith in Minden, LA, was interceding. Mom later told me that weeks before my birth, a woman in the Minden congregation paid the family five dollars to give me the middle name of Jerome, after the biblical translator and monastic leader, Saint Jerome.

Nine months prior to entering this earthly existence, prayer was fertilizing my ministerial future. With this spiritual preparation, it is no surprise I loved the Bible. Every book seemed like a letter to me. I carried a little Gideon in my shirt pocket as a source of comfort. Still, nothing about the ministry appealed to me as I looked at my dad's hectic life. Though my dad talked about family values, there appeared to be a disconnect: he was talking about family life but spending precious little quality time with his family.

I was twenty-seven when he died, and I had experienced feelings of overwhelm over the years. Where was Dad when I needed him to be present and listen to my Bible stories? Where was that fatherly voice of wisdom to guide me? Where was the mentoring to help interpret the confusing messages coming out of this contraption called "a radio"? Where was Dad for the scouting events and the sports instruction? Where was the fatherly instinct to teach his son how to be a man? When I looked back at my childhood and adolescence, I realized there were so many father-son rituals that were missing.

Most of our father-son conversations were dominated by his monologues. As a child, Dad's WWII battle scars had always piqued my interest. When I asked, "Where did you get that mark on your upper right arm?" he told me about his Army duty in France as an Intelligence Officer.

He said, "While we were on convoy in a Humvee, we were taking on fire from the Germans. I was under the vehicle and got grazed by a bullet. We were lucky."

Whenever we played table tennis, Dad spoke of his recreational exploits in France. Staff Sergeant Thomas was the 1944 military European champ in Table Tennis. Dad tried to maintain this skill throughout his post-military life. He often placed bets to see if we would be suckered into a game; he was sure to win. Dad said, "If you can get five points off of me, I'll mow the lawn on Saturday." This was his way of showing benevolence.

Dad's cancer allowed him to reflect and readily acknowledge his parental shortcomings. In his heart, he knew he had missed essential stages of his children's development. He acknowledged those parental failures and confessed them during the last year, 1980, before his death in March 1981.

As we finally sat together in the same bedroom, he was unable to move, and I was responsible for minimizing his movement. We shared what lay on our hearts. There was sadness in his eyes and voice. It was a different kind of authenticity that I rarely saw in him, face to face. Apparently, Dad had to slow down, to be honest with himself and me. As he propped himself in bed, there was a new humility about his spirit. The proud preacher, orator, and singer was humbled by his feeble ability to speak. In that humility, Dad finally heard my voice and became impassioned by my commitment to ministry. My brokenness resonated with his brokenness. In our common fractured status, we were able to hear the desires of our redemptive hearts.

Chapter Three

Swift to Listen, Slow to Speak

"So then, my beloved brethren, let every man be swift to hear,
slow to speak, slow to wrath."
James 1:19

From my sixth year to my twenty-first, I had a few conversations with my father. Unfortunately, most of our dialogue was a monologue initiated by Dad. I listened and obeyed. In our household, the parent spoke, and the child listened. This parent-centric style appeared to be the best way to keep my breeches from being inflamed. Dad had a temper, and I carefully kept my physical distance from his emotional fire.

I disliked the pattern of our father-son exchanges and dreamt that one day, I might get a chance to change our stale ritual. When I was nine, Mom went away to a Teacher's Conference in New Orleans. While she was away, my mind returned repeatedly to a passage in the book of Joshua. In chapter one, verse six, God commands Joshua, "Be strong and of good courage," and for emphasis, reiterates the command, "Only be strong and very courageous."

During that week, I had the opportunity to ponder these scriptures more prayerfully. Since schoolwork was a breeze and Mom wasn't around for conversation, I had extra time to meditate on the words spoken to Joshua. I decided on the Friday night before she returned, February 22nd, 1963, I would write a letter to Dad.

Dear Dad,

I miss you. When you are not here during the week, life is no fun. Ronita is too busy practicing her music and talking with friends, and Kelesha is too young to have a conversation with at five. She wouldn't understand my concerns anywhere.

So, I need you. We used to have time to play catch with baseball or football, but those days seem far gone.

What do you do all week? I hear a lot of things in the news and wonder if any of it pertains to you. Before you preach on Sunday and tell the church, could you give me some private time where you and I could share anything father-to-son?

I hope you aren't offended by this letter. It's just a small way of letting you know I miss you. I pray for you and want a few minutes of your time.

Love, your son

On Saturday morning, I woke up with the desire to turn my dream of a change between us into reality. I believed in my heart that a pivotal day had come. I jumped out of my twin bed, got dressed in blue jeans and a red plaid shirt, and walked past the sun-drenched window. With hope in my heart, I walked toward my bedroom door leading to the hallway.

As I approached the door, I heard unusual noises at the far end of the 40-foot corridor. The noises were so strange that I became apprehensive and feared opening the door. I cracked it slightly and peeked to observe the commotion. As I peered out, I saw my dad's anger in full wrath mode. What I saw, briefly, was him beating my elder sister, Ronita. He was standing over her robed body with a thin black belt in his hand. I quietly closed the door because I could not take the sight of this drubbing. It was too violent and harsh for my tender eyes. I could not imagine what Ronita could have done to deserve such punishment. She was extremely outgoing and expressive, a valuable sibling role model. She was gifted with musical ability, including the piano, French horn, oboe, and a voice like Diana Ross. Ronita was always surrounded by a chorus of friends who appeared to nurture her vivacious personality.

Though the door was closed, I leaned against the wall and listened for the belt to hit its mark on Ronita's flesh. As I listened for the whap, whap, I could not believe the tally. The whipping seemed to go on forever. I smelled the stench of bruised skin from the tattered leather strap. On that day, I made a conscious decision about what I needed from my father. Parental love seemed more important than discipline. I knew I was "a good kid" who didn't need the rod to understand the boundaries. Unfortunately, Ronita's humiliating punishment caused me to get a whooping from Dad. My desire to be noticed caused me to talk about the beating with others outside the home. Though there was pain on my bottom, every lick was worth the attention I got.

The result of that need affected my speech. I became silent, and that silence led to an atrophy of my linguistic ability. I was able to talk, but fluency was difficult. As a result, I felt embarrassed in public and kept quiet at home as it was better for my peace and survival; it was best to be spoken to rather than to speak. I eventually developed a verbal stammer that prevented me from saying my name with ease. I couldn't even say "Je…Je….Jesus" without stuttering. Any attempt to communicate got worse when I felt anxious. The positive aspect of not talking was that I developed a proclivity for reading. I preferred spending time by myself because both of my parents were college-educated and lifelong learners. There was a shelf of books and encyclopedias in the study. I spent a lot of time vicariously experiencing people, places, and ideas through reading. I was grateful for a place to explore and discover the world.

One of my most memorable times spent with Dad occurred when I finally mustered the courage to complain to him about my weight problem. During my junior year in high school, when I was 15 years old, I played Junior Varsity football. The summer before the start of that junior year, 1969, I realized I needed to gain weight, only to see it melt away a week later during strenuous football practices. That complaint turned into our Wednesday night milkshake outings.

I told Dad that it would be great if I could gain some weight since my thin 72-inch, 160-pound frame was taking a beating. Dad's strategy was to take me to Mel's Diner for a milkshake. I agreed to our meeting with cautious expectancy. Part of me could not believe the dream I had at nine would finally come true. Although I was dubious about the nutritional benefit, and somewhere in Dad's mind, he seemed to think drinking a milkshake would increase my aggregate weight. Of course, the lactic acid just made me sleepy, but I didn't want to tell him that. If I had told him, he might have stopped taking me for milkshakes, which would have brought our Wednesday night meetings to a halt. So, I kept quiet and kept the truth to myself. That was one of many emotional *"letters that I never sent."*

Ironically, the most painful incident in our relationship occurred at the end of those Wednesday "milkshake" rituals. It happened at Christmas, three weeks after my 16th birthday, in 1969. It was a thought-provoking scenario. My parents called me into the living room on the second floor of our five-floor home in the hills of Oakland and asked a question that pierced my heart. "Why don't you ever ask or invite any of your friends over to the house?"

As soon as I heard the question, I felt my heart strangely warmed, and tears rolled down my cheeks. It was not the question that brought me to tears but the pain of having to live with the tension around friendships since I was five years old. My parents had no idea the emotional turmoil they had created with their double messages about friendships. During the first ten years of my life, my parents insisted, "Never talk to white people, or you might end up dead like Emmett Till." Emmett Till was an African-American teenager who was lynched in Mississippi at the age of 14 for reportedly flirting with a white woman. So, I kept my mouth shut because I thought I might be the next lynching victim.

In Louisiana, I was surrounded by segregation wherever I walked. I drank out of "colored" water fountains, followed signs that read "colored only," and always sat at the back of the bus. Amid these second-class experiences, I sent a letter to my heart. I told my heart to help me live long enough to remove ignorance and educate people on the equality of the heart. Help me to be strong and of good courage as I fight the daily experiences of systematic racism. Give me the resilience to stand on your Word without fear.

Chapter Four

Looking for a Role Model

*"Your word I have hidden in my heart, That I might not sin
against You."
Psalm 119:11*

I would have given a small fortune to have quality time with
Dad during my childhood. I dreamed of having him wait on me
hand and foot. I prayed his presence would answer every question and read every thought that crept into my spirit. And my
mind was filled with anticipatory joy about how life would
change with fatherly guidance.

I imagined how Dad would have mentored me during the
Cub Scout years. I wondered if Dad knew anything about as-
tronomy. If he did, I wanted to ask, *"Have you ever seen the
Big Dipper, Orion's Belt, or the blood moon lunar eclipse?"* or
*"What did the sky look like while standing in a foxhole on the
third watch in France during WWII?"* If Dad answered, *"I saw
a yellow orangish flame coming out of the sky,"* I would follow
up, *"Was that mortar fire coming at you?"* I mused about the
endless possibilities.

I wondered if my baseball skills would have increased if
Dad had spent time hitting me hot grounders in the infield and
pop flies in the outfield. And as always, when I returned from
school, I yearned to hear him say, *"You up for some catch in
the backyard? I'll be Juan Marichal, and you can be Willie*

Mays." I was tired of playing right field; That's where they place people who can't play another position.

I wished Dad had shown me boxing techniques before the weekly tournaments in the church's fellowship hall. I yearned for a trainer to teach me the difference between a jab and an uppercut, a hook, and a cross. Those basic boxing skills could have prevented embarrassing defeats week after week. The constant smell of plastic from being knocked down was amplified by humiliation because Dad was the pastor and coordinator of the boxing competition.

Though it was occasionally a relief to romanticize what could have been, these fantasy scenarios with Dad never materialized. I craved a family member, friend, or television star to emulate, but no one emerged. Still, there was one family where I witnessed a vivacious father and son interaction. The Jarretts were an upper-middle-class African-American family with two sons and a daughter, and they lived in San Leandro, twenty miles away, though we had known them during my earliest years in Louisiana. The head of the household, Dr. Jarrett, was a cardiologist, and the mother, Norisa, was a schoolteacher. I befriended both the elder son, Cameron, and the younger, Warren. I saw Dr. Jarrett give his sons responsibilities—taking out the trash, serving meals, taking their place in doing the household work—and they reciprocated with caring attention to his instruction. Our annual family gatherings with them on long holidays continued for four years until Warren died of muscular dystrophy in 1968. Though these meetings were infrequent, I was deeply impressed, often moved, by the love shared between a loving father and his sons.

The Jarretts' example made me see that fatherly role modeling was possible and sustained some hope that I could have a similar relationship with Dad. I yearned for this feeling in his final days. After Dad's brain surgery in April 1980, we finally had a few intimate months together. During the hours I spent keeping watch in his room, he verbalized his dreams. He finally revealed what he had wanted to share for years. Dad spoke of his desire to move from the Senior Pastor's position at COAF to Pastor Emeritus. He wanted me to take over most of his ministerial duties.

At his funeral in March 1981, I realized all his dreams had evaporated when he died, and mine, as well. The father-son redemption that I thought would materialize vanished with his death, leaving me feeling like a Lone Ranger. *"Going it alone"* became my theme. I asked the Lord for direction but still needed an earthly mentor. I even approached Dad's prominent colleagues, but they appeared too busy. The demands of ministry left very little time to guide anybody outside one's congregation.

It's interesting to see how stories we take in as young children have an impact later in life. When I was very young, I had limited exposure to television; I wasn't allowed to see much of it, but I also thought watching visual entertainment was frivolous. I was more of a reader; television seemed to be a spectator sport as opposed to the real-life participation of writing a screenplay for television or a movie. Creativity was better than passive participation. Second, watching television was an earned privilege. With only one TV in our Louisiana home, we were restricted to what our parents wanted to watch or the siblings could agree on. Though I didn't watch much, there was one series I loved, *The Lone Ranger,* which aired from 1949 to 1957. The story was fictional, but it resonated with my life.

The Lone Ranger was so named because the character was the only survivor of a group of six Texas Rangers. I admired *The Lone Ranger* story because it had a moral message. My early years in our religious family were spent trying to find connections between the Bible and other stories.

As I read my little Gideon Bible at four years old, I noticed it was filled with precepts and laws. Some of the principles of

The Lone Ranger sounded like those discussed in the Bible. The Lone Ranger's creed said;

> *"That to have a friend, a man must be one."*
> *"That all men are created equal and that everyone has within himself the power to make this a better world."*
> *"That all things change, but the truth, and that truth alone lives on forever."*

The code appeared to coincide with some of the rhetoric I overheard in conversations about the Civil Rights Movement. Since I was too young to get involved in the struggle, I had to find a way to connect. The Lone Ranger appealed to my artistic desire to use metaphors from television to articulate feelings of injustice. Later, I was gratified to discover that the historical Lone Ranger was an African-American Marshal named Bass Reeves who hunted bad men and lived among Native Americans. This discovery became a lifelong motivator. No matter what I read or visualized in the media, I dug like an archaeologist until I found the truth behind the deception.

Like that ranger, I felt like a lone wolf, but I was not unfamiliar with isolation. Personal physical and developmental challenges forced me into years of relative solitude. Up to the age of seven, I had swollen adenoid glands, which blocked my ability to hear properly. In their effort to find a compassionate teacher who understood my hearing impairment, my parents moved me from school to school. As a result, from the age of ten to twenty-one, I had a speech impediment.

It's hard to forget the vow I later made in Kenya. I prayed, "Lord, if you heal my speech impediment, I'll serve you." I didn't know how this vow would manifest, but it finally resulted in a call to ministry. Twenty years later, after Dad died and my dream of ministering with him was dashed, I was presented with a second chance to pastor COAF.

On August 3rd, 2001, Rev. Snell, who replaced my father, also died. I pondered what Rev. Snell's death meant. I ruminated over my feelings for two weeks. Finally, as I drove into Alameda on a Thursday night for my Navy drill weekend, I was determined to act on this second chance. At three a.m. that Friday morning, I woke up compelled to express the anguish in my heart. I picked up a pen and wrote on the hotel stationery:

Church of All Faiths

Dear Members and Friends:

First, I want to express my condolences to the Snell family. My heart is extended to those who are currently grieving. My prayer is that the Lord will be your buckler and shield during your hours of need.

Second, I praised God for the leadership Pastor Snell provided since his pastorate in 1981. I supported the church whenever his leadership allowed me to speak a word from the Lord.

Third, I believe it is time for the body of Christ to understand my intent. From a ministerial perspective, my objective is to assist the church in whatever capacity the leadership seems appropriate. Whether it is leading board meetings, planning sessions, Bible study, prayer meetings, or preaching, I will adjust my schedule.

Fourth, using the word *pray* as an acrostic.

P- Pray for self, family, and the body of Christ.

R- Restoration, and revival, personally and structurally in the church.

A- Act after being led by prayer, scripture, and the Holy Spirit's direction. *"Trust in the Lord with thine heart; and lean not unto thine own understanding, in all thy ways acknowledge Him, and He shall direct thy paths." Proverbs 3: 5-6.*

Y- Yield to the Holy Spirit and to Christ leading in your life and the direction the Lord wants to lead the church.

Fifth, it is not my desire at this time to be a pastor, but I will assist in an interim capacity as the church searches for a pastor.

Sixth, if you desire to contact me, I can be reached through several modes of communication: Work, Home, Pager, and email.

Seven, I prayed for peace as the church goes through this difficult period, *"And the peace of God, which passeth all understanding, shall keep your hearts and minds through Christ Jesus." Phil. 4:7*

Your brother in the service of our Lord and Savior Jesus Christ.

Rev. Dr. R J Thomas

I wrote and typed this letter but never sent it. My head said, "No," but my heart said, "Yes, I'll try." I was conflicted. I didn't want to die early like Dad, and I didn't want to disappoint Mom. The decision to interview and finally accept the pastorate at the Church of All Faiths changed the course of my life. This decision is a grounding point for this whole memoir, *The Letter I Never Sent.*

Chapter Five

Out of the Frying Pan

"I have been a stranger in a strange land."
Exodus 2:22b

The conflict I felt about pastoring Church of All Faiths was not my first conundrum. Earlier in my childhood, I faced an internal conflict that no one understood. During my first ten years in Louisiana, I attended all-Black segregated schools during the week and an all-Black church on the weekend. I never met a white person during that first decade, which created a void in my life. The tension I felt in my heartstrings prompted a poem entitled "Separate But Equal."

Separate but equal is how I grew up,
Separate but equal filled my daily cup;
From schools to stores, buses to businesses,
Early in life, I realized there were differences;

Colored versus White,
Dirty versus Clean,
Back door versus Front Door,
Why is the White man so Mean?
What did we do to create such hate?
Why do we have to segregate?
I must spend my life trying to educate,

or society will continue to make this mistake.

Learn all you can,
Be all you can be,
Educate the world,
So that others will see.
Everyone's blood is red,
Everyone's tears are clear,
Everyone's heart can be pure,
With love's foundation, I am sure.

I carried this vision of equality and interracial harmony to California. Here, I was given a fresh start. I felt privileged to be in a new state, a new city, and a new neighborhood without the overt racism of the South. There were no segregation laws to restrict my movements. I learned life could be pleasant if my family "stayed in our lane." Staying in our lane meant living in the lower economic demographic of the flatlands as opposed to a home in the hills. I knew my parents, starved for home ownership, would do everything they could to move to the higher-income real estate in the Oakland Hills.

With any move to a new school, I anticipated threats. Nevertheless, I entered that first day of school with excitement. I wondered if saber-tooth tigers were waiting in the dark or boa constrictors were hanging from the rafters waiting to choke me. That first day at Durant Elementary went pretty much as expected. During the first recess, a tall, Black fifth-grader named Tommie approached me on the basketball court. Tommie towered over me by six inches and fifty pounds. I couldn't believe he was in fifth grade.

He said, "If you care about your life, meet me after school by the entrance."

The rest of that day was filled with anxiety as I prepared for this saber-tooth named Tommie. That day might have been different if Dad had taught me a few boxing skills, but this was no time to flee. At five minutes after three, the six-foot bully was waiting.

He said, "This is my territory, and if you want this school, you're going to have to fight me for it." That day, I took my courage from that Joshua passage and said, "My purpose is not to take anybody's territory, Tommie; this is your school. You're the king of the jungle." With that, I picked up my backpack and ran home three blocks away. After telling Mom about Tommie's threat, she was determined to get us out of the flatlands. Though the bully was expelled soon after that and never returned to Durant, Mom was laser-focused on moving to higher ground.

After two years in the flatlands, my family relocated to the Oakland Hills. My first day of junior high was filled with culture shock. In three months, my social environment changed from 100 percent Black to 99 percent white. With that change, my parents reversed their directive from "Don't talk to whites" to "Don't talk to Blacks." My parents had no idea of the tension that swirled within me. I felt uncomfortable at my new, mostly white junior high school but at ease at my predominantly Black church. My parents forbade me to visit any Black friends from church during the week. So, every day, I was emotionally torn about whom to befriend.

While I enjoyed my white friends at school and wanted to trust them totally, my Louisiana conditioning said, "I need to be careful." Ten years of restrictive barriers had created prohibitions that were difficult to remove. When I associated with Black friends, I felt natural. But I had to ensure their alternative rites of passage with girls and drug use did not become my own. So, I decided not to bring either white or Black friends home for fear of parental disapproval. This deepening conflict felt like emotional schizophrenia. My inner turmoil appeared to be a microcosm of the racial friction I was observing on a national scale.

The Civil Rights Movement that began in 1954 was in full swing, causing Dad to reconsider his appearance. On first impression, Dad would be perceived as a very light-complexioned man with Creole and Mulatto roots from Louisiana. This "high-yellow" hue often found Dad in the crosshairs of the bigoted South when my brown-skinned Mom accompanied him. Because of Dad's skin color, many police officers in Louisiana thought my father was breaking the state's anti-miscegenation statute. Though Dad was a man who could have "passed" for white, he was committed to the civil rights struggle. His dedication led him to work during the week in Mississippi with Dr. Martin Luther King, Jr. from 1960 to 1963. Dad led the Voter Registration Drive in Shreveport, LA, where he pastored for seven years. His involvement, along with Medgar Evers' murder and the KKK's signature cross burning on our lawn, forced the family to move to California for safety.

The Movement brought up another conversation about hair-styles—to be hip and relevant required an appropriate look. Dad allowed me to change my hairstyle from slick, laid-down coatis to a free-flowing Afro. I was surprised that he soon adopted an Afro style himself, appropriate for his finely textured hair. Changing my hair was more than a style alteration. It brought heightened cultural esteem. I felt authentic for the first time since my culturally-deprived junior high years. It was a touchstone that would eventually guide me to live and work in Africa.

During those secondary school years, Dad never sat down to instruct me about growing into manhood. We never discussed sex, how to treat girls and women, or even dating etiquette. I thanked him for allowing me to buy my uncle's Corvair in 1970 but didn't understand why my parents sold that same Corvair a year later while I was away at college without asking me.

My last memory of a conversation with Dad when I was in college took place in front of our living room fireplace. My parents had no idea of my vocational direction in college. Though I majored in Agricultural Economics and Business Management at University of California, Davis, they had no idea of my internal drive, direction, or purpose. It appeared that they didn't really care if I had enough money for school. They didn't care that I had to carry three jobs to feed and clothe myself and pay for college expenses. They didn't care what problems I was having with my toxic roommates. They didn't even seem to care about my faith journey.

One day, out of the blue, my parents got into a conversation about my future. In a moment of frustration, Dad observed to Mom, "If the boy doesn't do anything else, he can always be a pimp." Mom didn't respond to Dad's comment. I stared at him, speechless. I didn't want to know how or why those words even rolled off his tongue. Shaking my head at the verbal abuse, I rushed out of the house,

That disparagement was followed later in the evening with a comment about my clothes. Dad asked, "Why don't you dress in something other than blue jeans and a pea coat?"

I wanted to say, *"Why don't you use one of your credit cards and buy me some clothes,"* but I did not want to incur the wrath Dad inflicted on my elder sister, Ronita. I had never forgotten the whipping she received in 1963, so I kept quiet. To this day, I have no idea where those remarks came from, but they stuck with me for years as my Dad's impression of me.

Chapter Six

A Love That Endures

"Behold, you are fair, my love!"
Song of Songs 4:1a

I spent some time licking my wounds from Dad's demeaning remarks. I looked for reassurance in relationships. During the summer of 1973, I found myself in an unexpected liaison. I snaked up Golf Links Drive one Saturday, looking for a party. Having made the tour of my usual Flatlands hot spots, I moved on, looking for a lively party in the Oakland Hills. I turned onto Royal Oaks Road and saw a few people standing at a well-lit double door, waiting. I parked, joined them, and entered the party without an invitation. After a few pleasantries at the front door, I made my way down the flight of stairs to a family room the size of a church fellowship hall with wide sliding doors. A strobe light shimmered on a group of dancers. In the middle of the pool of light, I noticed a stirring. I stopped and stared.

I watched a pleated red skirt twirl with inexhaustible energy. This female phenomenon seemed to have mastered all the dance moves of the 70s. Tall and svelte, she easily transitioned from the Hustle to the Bump to the Funky Chicken without missing a syncopated beat. The charisma of her body and inviting smile drew me to join the dancer's circle. Within two songs, I found enough courage to ask her to join me on the dance floor. I was relieved when she said yes. Her name was Yvette.

I was thrilled. Usually, at parties, I would "hug a wall" in embarrassment after my stammered introductions; however, this time was different. Yvette's short-cropped Afro and a broad smile lit up the room, calming my anxiety. I noticed all eyes were on us, and at that moment, I felt a strange kind of redemption in Yvette's arms. Two hours of fast movements interspersed with slow dancing endeared me to this whirling dervish. Yvette's eclectic ability to comprehend and discuss anything was exciting. Her active listening skills were conspicuous. When we talked face-to-face, I insisted she remove her glasses as I didn't want to miss one nuance in her expressive face. Her dark brown eyes looked through me with fond admiration. Her close attention encouraged me to speak slowly and purposefully, with intention.

Yvette was the first person to genuinely listen to the rhythm of my heart. Her concern set a precedent for future relationships. When Yvette said, "Hello," there was a fresh sincerity in her voice. Her words drove deep and were layered with culture and theology. She could quote Shakespeare. She had read Bonhoeffer and Tillich. She knew what "redemption" meant.

Since seventy miles separated Oakland from Davis, quality time on the phone was critical. With this new relationship, my academic performance, as well as my energies, evolved. Economic theories that formerly seemed abstract suddenly jumped from the page. Histograms turned into romantic comparisons as I pondered the difference between Yvette and other women I had known. In the early evening, I'd call her.

"Hi, Yvette, how was your day?"

"Fine…glad to be home, hearing your voice. How was yours?"

"Ok, the usual, dealing with these strange roommates, you should see them."

"How so?"

"They do the most shocking things, especially after dinner. They get hilarious joy from lighting farts."

"What?" (She asked in shock.)

"Yeah, especially after eating some gaseous dinner like chili. They all get on the ground with their butts in the air, competing for a gold medal."

"What do they do?"

"With a lighter in one hand, they try to synchronize the gas from their butt with the flick of their thumb."

"Grotesque."

"Yeah, it flares about two to three feet. This must be a white-guy thing. I've never seen or heard anything like this before, and it stinks!"

"Thanks for warning me!"

"Oh, they would never do that in front of you, though they would think about it for a laugh. But moving on, what's happening in the Oakland schools?" Yvette was a teacher in the district.

"Trying to push students past mediocrity, push their limits."

"Hope you're getting support from parents!"

"Well, you know That's always a problem. A lot of them are just no-shows."

"You had a supportive family. I'm sure you're using that as a template for working with those parents."

"Yeah, I was lucky to have both a mother and a father in the home. Since my mom was a former teacher, she knew what I needed. She also knew what I wasn't getting in the classroom."

"Caring fathers and mothers are important. When one is busy, the other can pick up the load."

That was how the conversations went. They tided me over from day to day, but face-to-face on weekends felt like heaven. Yvette's tender touch made me feel loved and appreciated. She encouraged me to match her attention. Our relationship was a dance. Our hearts were blending. Whenever Yvette spoke, I wanted to get up, put my right hand around her waist, and grasp my left hand around her right hand. We would waltz across the floor to relive that first night when our hearts stood still.

When we couldn't dance, we reveled in music from our favorite collections, the duet album by Donny Hathaway and Roberta Flack or Marvin Gaye's "Let's Get It On." We memorized the words and sang them to each other.

"You've got a friend…ain't it good to know, you've got a friend."

With Yvette, there was synchronicity that seemed angelic. I knew if I ever left this earthly plane and ascended into the celestial skies, the thought of her love for me would be my shroud. If eternity was my home, I was confident for one fleeting moment, I was loved.

Our relationship deepened when Yvette invited me for dinner with her family, the Fosters. Naturally, I said yes to this august invitation.

I was surprised when I finally met them, though her father, Marcus, the Superintendent of Schools for the Oakland School District, was utterly unpretentious. I was shocked to find a man so kind and thoughtful with the responsibility of fifty thousand students and two thousand teachers. I was humbled to sit in the presence of greatness and see him smile in easy conversation with family. Yvette's mother, affectionately called Abbe, was a jewel. She smiled and hugged me with sincerity, which caused my heart to melt. I felt that I had walked into the perfect family, rich in tradition and unconditional love. The Foster family fulfilled the ideals I was looking for and missing in my own family.

My mother asked, "Why do you spend so much time at the Fosters?"

I told her unashamedly, "They exhibit appreciation, nonjudgment, forgiveness, and love." This response silenced my mother because she knew nurturing words were not her forte.

Instead of creating a change in her attitude, she saw Yvette as a threat.

She frequently said, "I don't like you going out with girls that are older than you." (Yvette was fifteen months older.) Her disapproval never deterred me from giving my heart what it needed. My mother's behavior during my relationship with Yvette gave me another opportunity to become authentic.

I never imagined I would be thrilled to visit and see my girlfriend's parents. The excitement of driving home from Davis seventy miles away every weekend was not to see my parents but to see Yvette and her family.

Before I entered the Fosters' door, I could feel them interceding for my safe arrival. When I drove up into the driveway, I would sit in the car for a few minutes to gain my composure. I thanked God that I found a girlfriend who adored me, a father figure who was wise, and another woman who loved me as though I was her own son. I was excited but didn't want to appear desperate.

When I entered the Fosters' house, I knew my world would change. Yvette treated me like a king, and her mother treated me like the long-lost prince that her daughter had been searching for. Even Yvette's father grinned with a paternal smile of approval. Within seconds, Yvette was asking about my wellbeing. "Robert, how are you doing? How was your day?"

These were not perfunctory inquiries. Yvette's words were like a red carpet invitation. I stepped into this castle of heartfelt comfort, where I was a cherished guest. With all this love coming in my direction, my dream of family unity and communication had finally come true. I knew that "I had arrived" in a contemporary version of Camelot.

Chapter Seven

Come Ye Disconsolate

"To everything, there is a season, A time for every purpose under heaven."
Ecclesiastes 3:1

Just when I thought life couldn't get any rosier, Yvette invited me to spend the weekend in Watsonville. I asked, "What's the occasion?"

She said, "It's my birthday, and I can't wait to show you one of my favorite spots." Though I had lived in California since 1963, this was my first overnight rendezvous with a woman. I had to be careful near water because the ocean mist made my heart vulnerable. The last time I spent hours on the beach, I melted a girl's heart.

Yvette and I were past that infatuation stage, and if this relationship deepened, I would be on the verge of engagement. I knew my heart was running ahead of my head. At twenty, I was young, but Yvette's love was mind-boggling. Entering the Watsonville property in Yvette's VW hatchback, I noticed the sign, **"Welcome to Pajaro Dunes, your paradise on the coast."** When I got to our second-floor room, I thought, *"Everything in this bedroom is top shelf, 800 threads per inch count on the sheets, a ten-foot fireplace, well-furnished kitchenette, and an ocean close enough to dip my toe in."* My dreams of the French Riviera came to fruition at Pajaro Dunes.

I felt out of my league. I had never imagined staying at a place this luxurious on college wages. But Yvette was a working woman, and I had no idea if she had savings or if her parents had gifted this condo. I was too immature to talk about money, and in fact, it was none of my business.

The weekend was surreal. I didn't know if this relationship could get more fluid. We floated in the rhapsody of romance—touches, words of affirmation, gift-giving. The best part of our quality time was listening to the waves. The rhythm of the water matched the constant beating of our hearts. Weeks after that, on the last weekend of October, we remained in the afterglow of Pajaro Dunes.

With November 6th, 1973 a week away, there were no big political conflicts on the horizon. Election Day was an exciting time to be around the KDVS radio station. Since our signal strength was 13,000 watts, locals often listened to our reporting before viewing the national news. I left the station, moseyed to the coffee shop, and picked up my dinner favorites, tuna bagels and cider, before going to the library.

As I chewed, a news break came up on the TV that almost caused me to choke. *"Breaking Story"* flashed over the top of the screen: *"Dr. Marcus Foster, Superintendent of Oakland Schools, has been shot. Reports indicate he was assassinated by a terrorist group called the Symbionese Liberation Army."* Yvette's dad!

Oh My God! I tried to steady myself as my heart raced and my blood pressure rose. I was overwhelmed with numbness and sorrow. This was one of the saddest moments in my life. In less than a month, the pendulum had swung from the celebration of Yvette's birthday to the death of her father. She called, and I hastened to her side. Yvette appreciated my immediate response to her grief. At other times, music became our comfort. It soothed the unspeakable waves of emotion. We lamented as we sang,

Come ye disconsolate, where 'er ye languish,
Come to the mercy seat, fervently kneel;
here bring your wounded hearts, here tell your anguish,
earth has no sorrows that heaven cannot heal.

Abbe was surrounded by comforters, but I was the only person to console Yvette. This incident taught me how to journey with someone in grief. Though we were not married, our lives revolved around one another. When I could not make it to Oakland, Yvette came to Davis. We were motivated by intimacy, emotional need, and spiritual healing.

I first learned about the seasons of grief as I mourned with Yvette. Shock, denial, and despair were not stages but a spiral. I never knew when hurt, regret, loneliness, or depression would arise or leave. Our theme song at the time might have been the ballad by Lionel Richie, "Just To Be Close To You." We called each other every day, like newlyweds, just to check-in.

Yvette would ask, "Honey, how was your day? How was school?" I responded with excitement, telling her about the concepts I was learning in Agricultural Economics and Business Management. Then she asked, "Are you coming home this weekend?

If I said, "No," she said, "Then I am coming to see you. Tell your roommates to make some space at the dinner table."

When Yvette visited me in Davis, my masculinity points were off the charts. My three roommates, who thought I had zero skills with women, were surprised. I even sensed they were jealous. None of the women they talked about ever visited them. Yet, I was able to get Yvette to visit me anytime I wanted. After her second visit, I decided to travel to Oakland for our weekend rendezvous. My intimacy with Yvette created too much friction with my roommates.

Deep within my heart, I wanted Yvette to be my first and only love. Both of us defined and redefined what a relationship should be. The care and concern we had for one another's hearts was exceptional. We cared for each other's hearts the way a gardener cares for a bonsai plant. Daily, we pruned, watered, nurtured, and fed each other with essential, loving ingredients. We were not shy in expressing our wants and needs. Yvette epitomized everything good and pleasant. She was affectionate, her family appreciative, and I felt cherished. She was devoted to God. Everything about her made me happy. Yvette was the first friend and lover I had known. I never thought those two words could be synonymous. She brought infatuation, passion, rapture, tenderness, yearning, and zeal into every second of the day. On top of that, I loved that she was Black.

During the Black Consciousness Movement, it was important to practice what you preached. Being with a person of color established my authenticity with the community. Though everything was going well in our relationship, I felt unhappy about my career decision. I questioned whether I had enough spiritual substance to keep Yvette. I had doubts about my vocation, too. I had no idea what I wanted to do. I knew God had given me energy, but I didn't know how to channel it. Without a definitive direction, it was hard to think about a long-term relationship. I knew Yvette had big dreams, but I wasn't sure the bond we had developed would survive long stretches of time apart. Yvette required all my attention, but in the process, I had nothing left for my own heart.

Yvette left Oakland in August 1974 and entered seminary for graduate studies at the Interdenominational Theological Center, in Atlanta, Georgia. After two months, she sent me my first and only "Dear John" letter. She expressed her devotion to theological education, her need for commitment from somebody, and my unwillingness to discuss our future.

This was one of the worst days in my college career. It felt like a dagger had punctured my soul. I was sad, depressed, and disappointed. Because I had never experienced the combination of these feelings, I was dumbfounded. Reading between the lines of Yvette's letter, I gathered she was committed to a new seminary boyfriend. I realized that, because of her father's death, she needed a father substitute. I had no doubt Yvette was making the wrong decision, but I was not experienced with conflict resolution. I felt it was futile to change her mind.

When we later talked on the phone, I said, "I just want to be friends," but Yvette wanted me to say more. I was not mature enough to understand that my words had power. I moved on to other relationships, but the standard for love had been set. I knew if I ever found anyone like Yvette, I would handle the relationship differently.

Chapter Eight

Waiting in the Wings

*"Then the Lord said to me, 'You have seen well, for I am
ready to perform My word.'"*
Jeremiah 1:12

April 1975, I was still healing from the "Dear John" letter
I'd received the previous fall. I was grieving for the person I
thought was the love of my life. I had experienced heartache
for the first time. I didn't know how to respond.

In the process of recovery, I decided to quit dating Black
women. I said to myself, "If this is how relationships end up,
I'm through with sisters." Though my thinking was flawed, my
emotions were on alert. I was traumatized.

I had determined in my heart to be more careful about the
next liaison. Clubbing or going to neighborhood dance parties
was off-limits. The next relationship was going to be effortless.
I was going to go to parties in my own neighborhood. I wasn't
taking any risks.

I didn't date for nine months. Finally, I accepted an invitation from my long-time friend Anita. This party was a small
house gathering of six persons. I knew I would be the only person of color present. Since last September, my focus has been
on finishing my senior year and being the Station Manager of
KDVS. In that capacity, I supervised 65 disc jockeys and a staff
of five. I had no intention of flirting or showing interest in

anyone at this party. I really didn't care if I met anyone, but serendipity occurred. That night, a rose opened before my eyes, Mariam Rose.

After introductions, Mariam offered to play a board game. I had never played chess with a woman, so I tempered my competitiveness. Though I was rusty, I faked it because I knew muscle memory would kick in.

We didn't discuss romance, but this chess game was filled with sensual tension. Every move was tantalizing.

"What color piece would you like, Mariam?"

She said, "I'll take the white pieces."

I said, "Apropos, I see this is going to be more than a battle on the board. What has drawn you to this game?"

Mariam said, "During this past year in France, I learned artists used to sit drinking wine and discussing art techniques around a game of chess."

"Are you going to give lessons on French artists while we play?"

"I might if you can keep up!" She twirled her curls.

"I'm chivalrous. You start."

Mariam opened with a pawn up two spaces.

I mimicked her, a black pawn up two spaces.

She was wearing a burgundy blouse with pearls, hip-hugging black pants, and gold half-rimmed glasses.

She said, "Who do you like better, Monet or Renoir?"

"I prefer Monet—his brush strokes are more lively. And like this knight, I'm going to best your pawn!"

"Oh, you're trying to give me art lessons and school me in chess at the same time?"

"Whatever I can do to win your admiration!"

"While you're admiring me, I'm going to take your bishop."

"How spiritual of you. Makes me want to sing. Who's your favorite musician?"

Mariam said, "I'm loving Phoebe Snow, *Poetry Man*."

"Every song or a few selections…?"

"No, I like 'Good Times' and 'San Francisco Bay Blues.'"

"Are you from San Francisco?

"Yes, born and raised. I went to Lowell High."

"I was conceived in San Francisco, born in Louisiana, but The City spirit lives deep in my bones."

The rest of the night was a symphony of intimate interplay. Mariam was an engaging conversationalist. She was both knowledgeable and curvaceous. Standing five-feet-seven-inches, with light brown eyes, her sultry voice raptured the air. When she smiled, her rose-petal lips opened the veil over my wounded heart. In the weeks after that party, I spent most of my time with her.

April flowers brought May showers as I prepared to tell Mariam discouraging news. We met at The Coffee Shop after lunch. After sitting down, I took her by the hand. "Mariam, please don't be mad, but I got a letter from the Peace Corps."

"What did they say?"

"The letter says I've been selected to teach in Kenya, and I leave in August."

"Well, That's fantastic. It's okay—we'll weather this." Mariam's optimism calmed my fears as she prepared for my transition to Africa. Leaving her was difficult but necessary. Her education in art history helped me understand the past and its relationship to our present. I often went to her slide-show presentations on the Impressionists and the Renaissance. What she could see in a painting—layers of meaning, angles of vision—helped me not only see art more clearly, but other things too. She changed the way I looked at my photography and even at my own sentences.

My world prior to meeting Mariam was scientific. She encouraged self-expression and creativity and helped me build self-confidence and a sense of my own identity. Her tutelage helped me to journal as I prepared to travel half a world away

from my parents. I wished they could empathize with the growing pains of my heart. This longing came out in a poem, "I Wish
They Knew."

I wish they knew my heart's desire. The little sparks
that caused my fire;
The tiny words that meant so much, The love of God's
subtle touch;
They've barely known me since my birth. I longed for
them to understand my worth.

I was an experiential learner who realized life can only be
understood through first-hand experience. I yearned to learn
what was rich and lively about African culture. As a media advocate, I was tired of hearing negative news—local violence,
for instance, or corruption among the powerful—that demeaned people of color.

One popular bit of fake news of the 1970s was propagated
by the physicist and Nobel Prize winner William Shockley.
This jack-legged geneticist was known for his extreme views
and advocacy on race, human intelligence, and eugenics. He
claimed, "Black people are genetically inferior to white people
intellectually." I was incensed and determined to spend my life
proving these racist theories untrue. An alternative goal of my
Peace Corps Mission was steeping myself in African history so
a different truth could be told.

My journey was an opportunity to live out the promise of
my childhood poem:

Learn all you can, Be all you can be,
Educate the world, So that others will see,
Everyone's blood is red, Everyone's tears are clear,
Everyone's heart can be pure with love's
foundation, I am sure.

Before leaving for Kenya, my parents gave me a wonderful graduation present—a cruise on a Norwegian ship to the Caribbean. Though my parents and relatives were on board, this was a gentle way of loosening the apron strings. I was shocked to see how adventurous I became among two thousand strangers. On the first night of the cruise, Masquerade was the theme. I spoke with the Cruise Director, who gave me a Playgirl outfit to accessorize. I went to Aunt Bea and borrowed a leotard and two wigs. I put towels on my hips and blew up orange balloons to fill out my chest. That night, I walked into the showroom in a curvaceous black leotard, cufflinks, and platform shoes, carrying a champagne bottle on a tray. I received a standing ovation and won first prize in front of 800 people. I was a recognizable face for the rest of the cruise. My parents said nothing. My aunt was proud.

On August 13th, 1975, I started my Peace Corps journey. We flew to Philadelphia, left two days later from La Guardia, and headed for Africa. At our first stop, I walked down the stairs and kissed the ground in Monrovia, Liberia. I was ecstatic to finally have landed in Mother Africa. The next stop was Accra, Ghana, where we disembarked for two hours. Then Lagos, Nigeria, where we could not get off the plane because a coup was taking place. We stayed on the tarmac for two hours and watched people running and hiding and police wielding guns while the plane refueled. Our group of 33 Peace Corps Volunteers (PCVs) finally arrived in Nairobi after a 22-hour transport.

My responsibility as a Peace Corps Volunteer in Kenya was to teach high school agriculture. The white culture I had been immersed in from 1965 to 1975 motivated me to deepen my understanding of this continent. For the first ten-week period, we were acculturated to Kiswahili culture. This felt like boot camp from sunrise to sunset. Unfortunately, the PC staff misunderstood my jovial spirit. They thought I was a drug user. I quickly squashed those lies and persuaded them my exuberance was authentic.

Throughout orientation, one challenge was finding appropriate female companionship. The ratio of PCV men to women was 5 to 2. At the end of our language training, a rumor circulated that seven new female medical staff would be arriving. On the appointed weekend in November, seven of my fellow male PC colleagues gathered in our favorite hotel. With binoculars, we scoped them out, envisioning relationships as the seven of them stepped out of the van.

When I saw a blue-eyed, five-foot-five-inch blonde emerge, I thought, *"I am going to make that lady my girlfriend."* Letters from Mariam were already dwindling. One hour later, I introduced myself in the lobby. "Hi, I'm Robert. *Habari yako*? (How are you?) Welcome to Kenya."

She said, "Thank you, I'm Jasmine."

"Can I see you tomorrow?" She said yes.

When we met, I asked, "So, do you have a boyfriend?"

Jasmine said, "Yes, he'll be coming from Alaska in a few months." My heart sank, but I recovered. "Okay, I understand; I hope to see you at the upcoming in-service." Two months later, we reignited our friendship.

During the weekend training, we talked like old-school chums. I asked, "How was time with your Alaskan friend?"

Jasmine said, "He came, we talked, and decided to part as friends." My heart started to race because my chance had come.

"Are you coming to the dance tonight?" She said yes.

Later that evening, I finally danced with her. Jasmine moved effortlessly with natural rhythm and grace. I asked, "Where did you learn to dance like that?"

She smiled, "I've always danced free-form." What a joy it was to mimic her moves as she tried to mimic mine. We danced with a soulful synchronicity for two hours. I knew that was the beginning of long nights, dancing in the moonlight.

Chapter Nine

Against All Odds

"Against all odds, when it looked hopeless, Abraham be-
lieved the promise and expected God to fulfill it."
Romans 4:18a

Jasmine and I were committed to each other. Our mutual
love for dance and yoga was the elixir of our weekend rendezvous. The chemistry was strong. Our conversation was lively.
But communication about race was mute.

I know why I kept silent. At twenty-two, I was still grap-
pling with the differences between Euro-centric and Afro-centric thoughts. I didn't know my voice and believed exploring
this tension would escalate strife. Jasmine didn't have concerns
about interracial relationships. She observed, "Isn't it great
there's no discrimination in Kenya!" I responded, "Yes" to her
face, but my gut said, "Fool, you know better." I was torn between love and authenticity.

Kenya gained its independence from Great Britain in 1963,
but tensions persisted. A trained eye could see the subtleties. I
saw the microaggressions. I saw how people looked at us when
we danced close. Though I saw the stares, my mouth would not
open to disturb our euphoria. In the process of postponing what
needed to be said, I became disingenuous. We cherished each
other naïvely, as though our love was an exception to the rule.
I behaved with selective amnesia. Our happiness anesthetized

both the racism of the Deep South and the bias of the Wild West. I suppressed all memory of the racial trauma of my past.

Still, I was aware of the "double consciousness." In 1903, W.E.B. Du Bois, an African-American intellectual, introduced that concept in his book, *The Souls of Black Folk*. Du Bois defined double consciousness as ***"the struggle African-Americans face to remain true to black culture while at the same time conforming to the dominant white society."*** Having spent ten years in a segregated state and another ten immersed in the dominant culture, I was one person with two identities. I was a case in point, "two souls, two thoughts, two unreconciled strivings." I lived with a peculiar perspective, looking at myself through the eyes of others.

Through this distorted lens, I knew why I was attracted to this blue-eyed woman from Boston. I had no idea why she was attracted to me. I believe the essence of Jasmine's affinity was based on how men of color made her feel. On the other hand, my attraction to her was part of my "socialization."

I remember going to my first dance in seventh grade with two hundred students. I was the only Black present. On that September afternoon in 1965, I sent a letter to my heart, "If the percentage of Blacks doesn't change, I will probably end up marrying a white woman." Ten years later, that premonition seemed about to come true.

Dancing with Jasmine felt natural. Whenever the rhythm started, we would be the first couple on the floor. She never knew my self-fulfilling prophecy was unfolding. I was scared to talk about what was manifesting. So, instead of talking, I took Jasmine by the hand, patted the sweat from her brow, and embraced her with enough passion to make the elephant in the room between us disappear.

The elephant never disappeared, but we found new ways to recast our situation. Jasmine's spirit radiated peace. "Let's love everybody," she would say, "and if we send love, love will come back." Instinctively, I believed her message, but my traumatized past discredited this ideology. I didn't know how to peel this onion. I grappled to find ways to both reduce my trauma and remain receptive toward the new ways of understanding.

A relationship with Jasmine was antithetical to my earlier beliefs, but I was open to change. I was willing to try anything that did not resemble my parents' way of life. One critical concern was knowing there was cancer in my bloodline. My maternal grandmother and paternal grandfather had died from cancer in their fifties, as my father did later. I wanted to stop that generational recurrence.

I wondered what diet might increase my greatest chance for longevity. Jasmine's vegetarian lifestyle was a plausible option. Flies covered Kenyan meat markets, and it took four hours to tenderize the beef. Unsanitary conditions and self-care drove me into vegetarian eating. The change had the residual effect of establishing discipline. I felt if I could say no to certain food groups, I could say no to other temptations.

A second change was Jasmine's Hindu theology. Though she had a Christian background, recent experiences at an ashram had steered her in an Eastern direction. I was the son of a preacher, but college academics displaced my appetite for religious inquiry. I was desperate to improve my spiritual growth. Jasmine awoke my dormant spirituality and led me to rethink why I believed in Christianity. I was naïve about the impact her ideology was having on my psyche.

Since Yvette had decided to marry and Mariam had stopped writing, I moved on. Jasmine was the best option for a long-term relationship. Prayer and meditation sealed my commitment to this resolve. I sent a letter to my heart: "I'd give everything for this plan."

Though I was committed, I knew complications were on the horizon. I sacrificed previous notions of inner peace for this

paradigm shift. I told my heart I was ready to embrace new trials rather than face the depression of loneliness. I believed Jasmine and I were dedicated to a spiritual path, and we needed
community. We needed God's presence, grace, and love. We
found a healing salve in weekend rituals of restoration and renewal.

During the holiday season, events occurred that normalized
this time of year. Over Thanksgiving 1975, Jasmine's parents,
Harold and Lenore, visited Kenya. We dined at Nairobi's 5-star
Hilton without incident. With Christmas approaching, my parents surprisingly planned a two-week safari, paying for my expenses. After their arrival, Jasmine and I dined with them at a
restaurant I only dreamed about on my $200 per month PCV
stipend. I was grateful they got a chance to meet Jasmine.

With a travel itinerary in hand, my parents talked about the
photographic opportunities for the coming weeks. I went out
and rented a camera with a special long zoom attachment. I was
excited about the first stop, Treetops Hotel, because it was ideal
for sighting wild animals. We trekked to Meru from Nairobi
and arrived late afternoon. The group had an early dinner in
anticipation of a 5 a.m. start the following day.

When I heard a knock in the morning, I got up without my
customary flip-flops. As I stepped outside, I felt a sting on my
right sole. I didn't complain about the discomfort but hurried to
get ready. Unfortunately, the foot pain worsened so bad that I
told my roommate to tell the group to go on without me.

This pain was unusual. I investigated the pain by drawing a
tub of warm water. Dipping my right foot in the water escalated
the agony. As I sat on the edge of the bathtub, the pain traveled
from my sole to the ankle, up the dorsal side of my calf, towards
the knee, and heading north to my right quad. I reached for a
towel and made a tourniquet around my right thigh. Knowing
more pain would be coming, I hobbled to the front door and
started yelling, "Somebody, come quick, I'm dying." As I

waited, I prayed, "Lord, please make this pain go away; I'll do anything." As the pain headed toward my chest cavity, I thought, "If I don't get help, the pain, poison, whatever…is going to stop my heart." In five minutes, the staff came and carried me to the resort van. After two minutes, I passed out. I remember being helped to a place with the sign of a caduceus (medical staff). After laying on a bed, I passed out again for hours. When I woke at 10 a.m., Mom hurried towards me with Dad in tow. In the aftermath, the doctors said I had been stung by a juvenile scorpion. Fortunately, I was rushed to the infirmary for an antiserum. Though I didn't want the attention, the group treated me like a "rock star" for the remainder of the safari.

I believe the scorpion incident elicited greater understanding from my parents. During the two-week safari, they listened to my concerns when we visited Ngorongoro Crater and Olduvai Gorge, archeological sites of the "Cradle of Civilization." We talked about Genesis and the three-million-year-old "Lucy." They finally heard me. It was a blessing.

Chapter Ten

Pressing on the Upward Way

"I press toward the goal for the prize of the upward call of God in Christ Jesus."
Phil. 3:14

The safari trip answered lingering questions for my parents. These inquiries were not on the itinerary, but they needed attention. During my young adulthood, my parents doubted my industrious spirit. They gibed at me, "You won't know hard work until you pick cotton." During the safari, they came to my Taveta home, where they saw my garden. After seeing my well-developed farming skills, they never doubted my industriousness again. And my speedy recovery from the scorpion sting debunked the idea that I was a wuss.

With my parents' approval rating at an all-time high, I felt free to become serious about deep emotional connections. If you asked me before going to Kenya, "Would I travel one thousand kilometers per weekend to spend 32 hours to get to a woman I was courting, risking possible death? I would have responded unequivocally, "No!" but that was exactly what I did for sixteen months.

Every Friday afternoon, I traveled from Eldoro High School to Taveta, ten kilometers away, to catch the bus. The general store manager allowed me to keep my motorcycle hidden behind his establishment. At 4 p.m., the bus driver would shout, *Mimi kwa tayari* (I'm ready to board). I stood in line with my green duffel bag and watched passengers queue up. They carried food in sheets and babies wrapped in scarves. The auxiliary bus staff chewed a plant that looked like rhubarb leaves. I was told the plant had the medicinal effect of Meth. This drug kept them laughing, alert, and high throughout the night. I paid five shillings for the three-hour trip to Voi, where I transferred for another ten-hour trip to Nairobi. The journey was noisy, filled with Swahili chatter I could not decipher. I hardly slept, hoping not to miss my final stop at 5 a.m.

Then, I walked 10 minutes to Jasmine's apartment. I tiptoed to the entrance before entering. Jasmine always slept on a mattress on the floor. She welcomed me and said softly, "Come and lay next to me." I would oblige her request and thank God for the traveling mercies. I pinched myself and mused, "How did this relationship spiral up so quickly?" I never verbalized those thoughts but pondered them during our 32-hour weekend trysts.

One Saturday evening in the summer of 1976, as I walked to Jasmine's condo, I was approached by a Kenyan man. He spoke to me in Swahili. I thought he asked how I was doing. I said, *"Vizuri"* (I'm fine). For some reason, this man did not like my response and said, "I am going to kill you if you don't tell me who you are." He brandished a weapon that looked like a .22 caliber revolver from his belt and pointed it at my chest. I responded in clear English, "I am a Peace Corps Volunteer, teaching in Taveta." The assailant slowly tucked his gun back into his jacket. I paused to thank God for dodging another dangerous encounter.

My relationship with Jasmine continued for a year before we started talking about getting married. I don't remember proposing on one knee, but I recall in rich detail one rainy night in June after our first pastoral counseling session. The following is a reflection on the emotional complexities of that evening.

Today I Cried Again...

I should have cried with you on that dark rainy night,
I should have seen something in your spirit that wasn't right;

I should have sensed your monsoon of fears,
Should have been intuitive about our frontier;

I should have detected lightning in your soul,
Downcast eyes signified trouble in our hole;

I should have seen the confused missteps,
Felt the shallowness of our depth;

I heard your thunder; you never held it in,
Static charges hit like a whirlwind;

I cried again, not with an external tear,
But an internal drip that kept me present and aware.

Two months later, we discussed the rainy night concerns and resolved to press on. I opened my ears on Saturday morning, August 27th, and heard a minor bird's mating call. I saw the male jump from branch to limb on a flaming acacia tree. The tree's bright blossoms dimmed in comparison to the plumage displayed by this chirping fowl.

I also yearned for attention from my betrothed. I twisted and turned to ensure Jasmine touched my torso. She touched enough to satisfy the longing we both felt.

"What do you want for breakfast?" I whispered.

Jasmine reached out with her fingertips beckoning me, looked up, and softly said, "Oatmeal and fruit salad."

We hugged for the last time as single folks, smiling with sweet satisfaction. We also sighed, realizing we had a lifetime to fulfill our dreams. It was the last embrace before our wedding day.

I rose to fix breakfast as Jasmine prepared for morning meditation. I put the kettle on, opened the sliding door, and spread my fingers to shield my eyes from the bright morning beams shooting through. I picked up the papaya and scraped the black seeds without removing the meat inside. Then, I selected the ripest mango. I cut the mango, and sweet juice ran down my fingers, symbolizing, I thought, the sweetness of our union. I glanced over and saw Jasmine smiling from a happy thought in her own trance.

As Jasmine lifted her hands, I knew meditation was ending. I moseyed to the bed and asked, "How was your time?"

She said, "Peaceful and energetic…I feel motivated to handle what lies ahead."

Jasmine's words prompted me to pick her up and place her in the breakfast nook. Before our meal, I prayed, "Lord, bless our pending marriage as we prepare for the greatest day of our life. Let all we do glorify you. Amen."

We ate quickly and listed the cleaning items needed for the day's task. Buckets, sponges, long-stemmed brooms, Mr. Clean, towels—check! We seemed ready to clean the chapel. But I wished we had made a list of the ingredients necessary to keep our hearts cleansed. It was going to take more than dance, yoga, and vegetarian diets to keep our marriage afloat.

With our last bite, I gathered the dishes, saying, "You get dressed while I finish cleaning up." I took the keys to the green Volkswagen and packed cleaning items in the back seat. Jasmine winked from the bathroom, her sign that she was ready. As we started on the Narok Road toward the Chapel, unpleasant thoughts intruded.

Her post-counseling crying episode haunted me. The drama of that night made me feel hesitant, though not hopeless, to the point of calling off the wedding. Still, there was uncertainty in my spirit. I wondered if a similar episode would happen again. Clearly, Jasmine had the capacity to get upset. She was well in touch with her emotions. But I was doubtful about my own. I'd never expressed a full range of emotions with someone I loved.

I thought, "Maybe I just have premarital butterflies or jitters as couples do." I never told Jasmine about these musings in my heart for fear she would not understand.

We arrived punctually at noon to clean the Mai Mahiu Catholic Church. I cleaned with anticipatory happiness, knowing that tomorrow the work would be over. I didn't realize the real work of marriage was just beginning.

I was, though, a little unhappy with the thought of having to labor so hard the day before the wedding. I knew how moody I got when tired and hoped that moodiness wouldn't show. I didn't know how Jasmine would react if she saw me moody just before our wedding, so I stuffed my feelings. It didn't matter how exhausted I was; this was no time to show weakness.

I knew how difficult the task was to clean Dad's church. This was the dirtiest floor I had ever washed. Rat and bird droppings were everywhere. I was familiar with marbled surfaces, but this floor took my exhaustion to a new level. I thought if I was tired, I could only wonder how drained Jasmine was likely to be.

We worked side by side, scrubbing and cleaning. The chapel gardener dropped by, looked at us, and scratched his head. It had been a long time since he'd seen anyone cleaning that chapel. As I cleaned, I fantasized about our wedding night. With each scrub, I wondered if I would have enough sexual energy to consummate the marriage. I knew the effort we were exerting would hamper the fun.

We wished we had come on Friday or the weekend before to clean. Some of the spots were impossible to remove, but we did our best. Finally, when the sun was fading over the Rift Valley and the chapel was growing dark, we knew it was time to stop. We looked at each other and acknowledged, "That's good enough." We double-checked with each other: "Is that okay?" We had cleaned the entrance until it shined. Sometimes, okay is good enough. Driving back, we were exhausted but satisfied. I prayed we would have this same dedication when it came to resolving blind spots in our marriage.

Chapter Eleven

A Leap of Faith

"Now faith is the substance of things hoped for, the evidence of things not seen."
Hebrews 11:1

The first thought on our Wedding Day, August 28th, was, *"I need to talk with Dad."* My father had shown me a picture of a German woman he almost married during WWII in France. I wanted to understand what had flowed through his mind as he pondered that possibility. I needed counsel on entering this union with a clear conscience and without regrets.

I awoke on this sacred Sunday with a familiar housemate. Jasmine stayed at her girlfriend's house, but Ali Rico stayed with me in Nairobi. Rico had been my housemate in Taveta for the past thirteen months. He had witnessed my journey and was the reason I was still alive.

Nine months earlier, life had looked grim. One agonizing night, I lay on an 8 by 10-foot bed with a high fever in a pool of sweat. Guilt filled my mind. *"Why didn't I listen to the advice about Quinine? Why didn't I sleep under a mosquito net?"* Malaria was real. Rico checked on me at 6 p.m. and took my temperature, which was registered as 102 degrees. He left, saying, "You'll be alright in the morning. Call me if it gets worse." In an hour, fatalistic thoughts raced through my mind. *"If the fever doesn't go down, this twin bed will be my final resting place."* I lay motionless for hours, pondering my death. Weak and dehydrated, I mused, *"I know God wants more from me. I don't believe the Lord brought me eight thousand miles to die in a bat-infested tin-roof shack. If this fever persists, I'll be going home in a pine box. Maybe the school will bury me in the graveyard outside my door."*

In desperation, I made a vow. "Lord, I'll turn my life over to you if you get me out of this predicament. But if this temperature gets higher, I won't have any brainpower left. Lord, my brain cells are frying, and I'm losing prefrontal activity." I needed help, phasing in and out of consciousness. Where was Rico? My voice weakened with each minute. I screamed, but Rico couldn't hear my anguished cry. In a moment of divine inspiration, I threw a coin at the door and shouted, "Rico!" I tossed another higher and shouted again.

Finally, on the third try, I aimed the heavy Kenyan shilling at the opening above the door. I heard scurrying, and Rico appeared. It was midnight. *"Namna gani, bwana"* (How are you doing)?" "Fever, hot, weak, need *dawa* (medicine)." Rico was only five-feet-six, but his gentle spirit was giant. Like a combat medic pulling a wounded soldier out of a foxhole, he dragged me to the infirmary, a quarter of a mile uphill. The nurse found some powerful medicine, and the fever, by then 105, subsided. I was grateful that I had a roommate that night. Living with another person, even though it means forfeiting some privacy, can pay dividends.

The jitters over matrimony remained, but Rico's presence brought peace. I was sad my friendship with him was coming to an end. He was the best housemate I'd ever had. I would miss his strength of character and calm demeanor. As Jasmine and I exchanged vows, I promised to "be faithful, for better or worse, in sickness and in health, till death do us part."

Though Jasmine and I had romanced each other for sixteen months of weekends, there were times we still acted like strangers. We cared for each other, but the relationship felt weak in tense moments. During verbal conflicts, the large deposits of compassion in the vault of tenderness dwindled.

The wedding night was not what I had hoped. After our reception, we drove an hour to a resort in the Rift Valley. Jasmine told me on the way to the resort that she had picked up a parasite in the soles of her feet. My dreams of a blissful night were crushed as I spent the evening caring for Jasmine's heart and infected feet.

Thirty days after the wedding, we moved to the western section of Kenya. We migrated to Luo country, where the second largest tribe in Kenya lived. Most of our time had been spent with the dominant Kikuyu tribe in Central Kenya. The Kikuyu tribe was resented for several reasons. They dominated the economy. They drove the matatus and taxis, ran the newspapers, and constituted most of the civil service jobs. They accounted for 22% of the Kenyan population and functioned with "entitlement" the Luo didn't share. The Luo, however, were friendlier people.

Jasmine and I traveled west up the tarmac—their term for the road—concerned about the personal belongings we had sent ahead. We didn't have much, but what we had made Kenyan living bearable.

"Another leap of faith," I said.

"Yes, we'll see if fortune is on our side. Don't know, Rob, I have a funny feeling about this new place."

"What feels different, tribe or location?"

"Not sure. I have traveled so much for the Catholic Relief Services, I've developed a sixth sense about places."

"That's an intuitive side you've never revealed."

"Yes, I guess that's part of marriage — new things come out of nowhere."

I smiled, thinking, *isn't that the truth*, but said, "Feel free to keep sharing. The more I know, the closer we'll become."

Jasmine's smile gathered wrinkles at the corners of her eyes. We poked fun at each other's facial nuances that kept us laughing. When we got bored, we pointed out the differences between coastal beaches and hilly terrain. We noticed the increase in the secretary bird population, huge birds the size of wild turkeys, and snake predators, which meant snakes were plentiful.

Traversing the tarmac, we were lost. Our new school wasn't even on a map, but we had a name. With Jasmine's fluent Swahili, we were confident we would find our way.

Our new home was located near Lake Victoria. Prior to our arrival, the headmaster had promised adequate housing. Over the phone, he guaranteed a safe, secure home within walking distance of the classrooms. In person, his dishonest face and boastful assurances made us feel skeptical. We both felt there must be something wrong.

At this new school, Jasmine's role involved teaching health care and nutrition to mothers. My role was preparing students for the high school equivalency test in agriculture. Having fulfilled our initial two-year Peace Corps commitment, we were happy to extend our contracts. It was a joyous time to live out our hopes and dreams. We looked forward to working and living at the same location. This move was our ideal, living in the land of picturesque sunsets and unforgettable sunrises.

In September 1977, Jasmine and I settled on the grounds of Kaibondo High School. To heighten our expectations, the headmaster informed us our residence was formerly owned by the farm hand for the Minister of the Interior. Through the front door to the farmhouse, there was a long walkway leading to the only bedroom. The living space was filled with a king-size bed, mosquito netting overhead, and a large kitchen, complete with a refrigerator and breakfast nook. This looked like a perfect respite after a long day of teaching and helping mothers in the community.

Jasmine and I relaxed after our long day and fell asleep to the noise of mosquitoes buzzing near the surface of our netting and hopeful crickets chirping outside. But after two weeks, my beloved noticed an unfamiliar sound.

Jasmine said, "Did you hear that?"

I said, "No."

"Listen, it's coming from that direction over there!"

I turned my head toward the eight-foot white vertical post where her eyes were fixed. In the dim light of the kerosene lamp, I could see faint movement. As I inched closer, I could not believe my eyes. Insects stirred up, down, and sideways across the column. They were larger than fire ants, with particles in their pincers. These nocturnal creatures looked like termites. I tried to sleep, but the noisy wood-feeders kept me up. I had to stand watch for the family against this constant threat.

The next morning, Jasmine woke up extremely agitated. She yelled with frustration, "I can't live here anymore. I can't live with termites in the bedroom. This is awful, dangerous, and unsanitary!"

As I listened to Jasmine's outrage, my stomach churned. Digestive juices worked overtime as I listened to her angst. Each day, I internalized the pain and suffering she exhibited. Whenever she frowned, flared her nostrils, or dropped her eyes to the ground, I took responsibility for our infected farm home. My stomach balled up like a threefold cord of sisal rope. Jasmine's sixth sense and my conflict aversion eventually came to a head. The emotional strife was so intense it impacted my ability to stand. As a result, I could no longer teach. Though the infestation was not my fault, I blamed myself. The guilt of putting my bride in danger lodged in my internal core. The marriage was facing its first major crisis.

Chapter Twelve

Being Slow to Anger Is Better

"A soft answer turns away wrath, But a harsh word stirs up anger."
Proverbs 15:1

The stress of the termite infestation brought teaching to a halt. After the first ten minutes of eating, digestive juices caused gastric pain that zapped my ability to stand. The Peace Corps sent me back to Nairobi for a medical diagnosis. Test results indicated a spastic duodenum. No amount of organic yogurt, oats, or carrots alleviated the pain. The only relief came from taking a prescription drug called "Tagamet."

We had a choice. No other housing was available. We had to live with termites or leave our assignment and return home to the United States. Jasmine and I decided on the latter. It was the only option for the well-being and survival of our marriage.

Honestly, I had been irritated from the outset about the whole move to Kaibondo. I was frustrated that I couldn't keep the promises I made to students and upset that I had put Jasmine in danger. The entire situation cut me to the core. This deep disappointment decimated my physical, mental, and emotional resilience. My intuitive self was challenged and in need of repair. I had become dependent on medication in a way I never would have chosen. I distrusted Big Pharma. I wanted to live a holistic life, eat healthy, and remain drug-free. I sent a letter to my heart, "Never be dependent on medications to control my gut health. I must find alternative coping techniques."

So, over the next few weeks, we packed up our belongings and made plans for the transition back. We were again disappointed. Kenya has given us such joy and so many once-in-a-lifetime moments. This country that had brought Jasmine and me together would soon recede into our past. Our time there would be part of our story but not day-to-day discovery.

During this disappointment, I sent ultimatums to my heart. "Never override my clear intuition when making decisions. Never make a move without asking hard questions about particulars. Never sabotage my own dreams with false diplomacy. Never let conflict avoidance cause mental and physical anguish. Never have another spastic duodenum. Heal and adapt."

We left Kenya at the end of November 1977 and headed back to America by way of London. We wanted to pass through Cairo, but there was too much unrest in that region. We prayed the heavy fog in London was not a bad omen for our future. Our first stop was Long Island, New York where we stayed for a few days with Jasmine's sister.

Arriving in New York was our first experience as a couple in America. I immediately noticed differences. Interracial and inter-tribal couples were completely normal in Kenya. I forgot that interracial marriage had been legalized by the Supreme Court only in 1967. When we returned, the subtle leers we had received in Kenya turned to blatant, sometimes hostile stares. Most of them came from African-American women. "Can't a brother date his own?" they seemed to be saying under their breath. Their gawking felt mean-spirited and unforgiving, but they were my sisters. Despite this animosity, we continued to profess our love. We believed all things were possible if we kept the faith.

Every month presented new challenges. Christmas 1977 brought another round of marital disagreements. Jasmine decided to stay in NYC so she could visit her parents for the holidays. I decided to go home to California to be with my family. Though I originally thought this was a good arrangement, our decision to separate over the holidays turned out to be a terrible idea. I didn't understand the importance for her, or even for me, of being without the one you love for the holidays.

Back in California, I was homesick for my bride. During Christmas dinner, I sat on the carpet and ate from a coffee table. In Kenya, sitting on the ground was such an acceptable posture that it became a natural place to put myself. While others sat in chairs, I sat yoga-style alone. My separation was intentional because no one there could relate to my experiences. No one understood or wanted to hear my critical thinking about either Africa or America. I felt like the lone wolf again. The conversations my relatives were sharing seemed trite compared to the life-and-death experiences of my previous two years, and I felt alienated being at a gathering without Jasmine. She was my family now.

So, I moped around for two weeks, waiting for Jasmine to arrive in the Bay Area. After she arrived, we stayed at my parent's house for a couple of weeks until we found a place to rent. I was surprised my parents planned a reception for us at the church after the service. This was a good sign they were going the extra mile to accept Jasmine. Because of her affinity for vegetarian cuisine, we looked for apartments in Berkeley, where vegetarian restaurants seemed to be on every corner. Our goal was to be near the Food Co-op to ensure the purchase of the freshest organic food. We found a great location with a bohemian vibe near Alcatraz Avenue, about a mile from the university campus.

The next move was to find employment. Nurses were always in demand, and Jasmine had a plethora of choices. She got a job within three weeks at Alta Bates Hospital in Berkeley. I sent another message to my heart. "In the future, pursue a job and career where you will always be in demand." Because we only had one car, I picked her up from the evening shift at 10 p.m.

For three months, I sent resumes detailing my training in economics and business management to companies every day—banks, businesses, and PG & E—and got one interview every couple of weeks. In the third month of my search, Jasmine said something insensitive. While standing in the living room near the kitchen, she said, "Where's your initiative and motivation?"

She seemed to have no idea what effort I was putting out to get a job. The ease with which she found employment gave her no empathy for the hiring discrimination I faced. Jasmine's lack of empathy pissed me off. One thing I hated was being perceived as lazy or indifferent about work. Jasmine's comment was an assault on my manhood and ethnicity. She broke the cardinal rule of "What not to tell a Black man." I was incensed and wanted to hit her. My bowels hollered, "How dare she accuse me of lacking initiative!" I felt my amygdala disconnect from my reptilian brain. Rage at the insult filled my body with pent-up anger. I was ready to explode.

Fortunately, at the moment of her verbal abuse, I was sitting in a lotus position at our round dining table. Sitting allowed me to reflect on the reactions running through my head. Thinking about hitting Jasmine made my whole life flash before my eyes. I knew if I hit her, I would be charged with domestic violence, and that act would affect every future hope and dream. Striking her was not an option. I proceeded to do something I had never done before. Instead of hitting my wife, who was standing, I turned ninety degrees and put my right hand through the living room wall. Surprisingly, the force of my hand shattered the wall, leaving a hole five feet wide.

Jasmine looked shocked. She asked, "So, what are you going to do about *that*?"

I said, "Go to Ace Hardware, get some plaster of Paris, a spatula, a putty knife, and repair the wall."

This incident caused me to make another promise. I sent another letter to my heart: "I will never allow anyone to take me to the brink of physical abuse." Coming so close to it made me aware that I might have an anger management problem. Did I carry the generational trauma of my father, or was my reaction a normal response to a hurtful remark? This was the first time I realized how the words of another could make me sabotage my best self. I said to myself, "Never again would you allow yourself to be placed in a situation to become a domestic violence statistic." I prayed, "Lord, there must be a better way." This incident was a gut check for my spirituality. Had my "inner man" fallen so low that I was allowing words like hers to disturb my inner peace? I had been employed since I was 15 years old. I couldn't let this dry spell, frustrating as it was, affect my self-esteem. I was better than the reactive person I had recently become.

I dropped Jasmine at work, glad I had dodged what could have been a life-altering confrontation. Driving to the hardware store, I was relieved that wisdom and discernment had prevailed. During difficulties like these, I learned that when you're going through hard times, life moves slowly. When life is pleasurable, years float by. I looked forward to fair winds and calm seas for the future.

Chapter Thirteen

Nose Dive Pending

"Has God forgotten to be gracious? Has He in anger shut up
His tender mercies?"
Psalm 77:9

After that hard moment with Jasmine, I felt like an airplane out of control. My self-esteem was deeply threatened. After three months of spiraling downward, I finally found employment. I took a job in Sacramento, 80 miles away. It was an act of desperation. I didn't like spending three hours a day on the freeway, but I was at peace. Being employed gave me a sense of normalcy. I gradually stopped hearing "lazy" on an internal loop of accusation.

I accepted a position as a Graduate Research Associate with the State of California Agriculture Department. The job involved testing moisture meters at every licensed site. Meters are used to measure the percentage of water in grain. I was assigned to test and calibrate every known meter. Apparently, non-calibrated meters were unfairly charging grain producers, and hopefully, my testing would resolve that discrepancy.

When I was home on Sundays, Jasmine and I tried to enjoy life. We spent time at the beach near Golden Gate Park or Ghirardelli Square. I thumped the conga drums as Jasmine creatively danced. The drumming was a distraction from the real beat of my heart. I needed the spirituals of my youth to reconnect the faith, hope, and struggles of my life. Every time I suggested going to church, though, the invitation fell on deaf ears. Jasmine further balked at the idea of seminary training. I decided never to broach that issue again, but she knew my desire.

As we accustomed ourselves to life with each other, we also hyphenated our names, which I thought I'd never do. I became Robert Bloom-Thomas. This felt weird, but it was the chic thing to do in the 70s.

The Sacramento job was the worst job I'd ever had. Every town felt like the armpit of California. I sensed God put me in straits, as though He was saying, "Try it your way, buddy; I'm going to affect every part of your life until you surrender." When I was supposed to be in the field, on weekends, I'd sneak home to be with my bride. This job dismantled sixteen months of carefully nurtured intimacy. After two months, Jasmine found alternative employment. She joined a medical group that traveled throughout the state, administering care to farmers and low-income laborers.

We had never been apart from each other for more than a week at a time. Jasmine had the family car, and I had a state vehicle. Scheduling conjugal visits on the fly was impossible. This scenario lasted six months before we decided to give up our toxic lifestyle. We needed stability and daily contact to survive.

California living had proven too difficult, so we moved to Massachusetts to try our luck in Boston. We left our west coast jobs in October 1978 and trekked east. Our first stop was to see Jasmine's parents in York, Pennsylvania. Jasmine's father, Harold, was the CEO of a refrigerated freight company. At the Blooms', I was able to watch the father-daughter interaction. We stayed only two weeks, but I saw the irritations Jasmine had shared. Harold offered me a job at his company, but I couldn't envision working for him. This was not my dream.

The only thing on my vision board was fulfilling the promises I made to God. Malaria bouts, scorpion stings, and attempted assault had humbled me. The last Sunday of November, we attended Church on the Rock in York. I don't remember the sermon title or scripture reading, but the theme was "surrendering to the call." During our courtship, I had mentioned there was "a call" on my life. I didn't know how it would materialize. After the sermon, the choir sang, "I Surrender All." That hymn drew me to the altar. I confessed before the congregation, "I have been running from God for a long time. Like Jonah, it's time to relinquish all power to Abba Father." That public confession was pivotal. We never returned to that church, but Jasmine heard my true commitment.

We left York and headed to Boston. On black ice, we traveled to stay with one of Jasmine's male friends. I was skeptical when Jasmine talked about her male friends because I suspected she had been intimate with these fellows. Cautiously, I looked for opportunities to leave to find other accommodations.

In my desire to follow my calling, the devil was busy. As we strolled the streets of Boston, we stopped by the Hare Krishna Temple. We were not unfamiliar with the Hare Krishna philosophy, having visited their temple in Nairobi. We stopped by on a cold Sunday after the Martin Luther King, Jr. holiday. We eventually moved to the Hare Krishna house in Boston. The house was a three-story building with a long stairway. We carried our meager belongings and clothes up three flights of stairs into our new apartment.

I felt out of place. What was I doing in a Hare Krishna temple three thousand miles from home? I was as far away from the Christian community as I could imagine. We got up every morning at 3 a.m. and tried to do 16 rounds of Hare Krishna repetitions on our prayer beads. This practice is similar to Catholics praying the rosary. Every morning after breakfast, we did menial work and hit the streets trying to get converts. I never pulled my hair into a ponytail, but I trimmed my beard. I loved the food and enjoyed playing the drums and dancing in the worship hall. But I totally detested the worship they gave to idols. They put garlands around miniature statues of Krishna and offered food to similar idols. I remembered the Ten Commandments, the first of them being, "You shall have no other gods before me." Jasmine had made her peace with the household and its practices, but I lived with growing ambivalence and discomfort for weeks.

Every time I participated in worship, I knew my actions were a direct violation of the commandment. Engaging in this activity was extremely disturbing. My soul, mind, and spirit got violently sick, and I ran a high fever for a week. I did not chant and barely ate any Krishna-offered food during that illness. I was grateful Jasmine was a nurse and knew how to keep me hydrated during my convalescence. After living in the Hare Krishna house for a month, we knew it was time to move on. During that final week, we looked for another living situation.

After combing through advertisements for home rentals, we drove to West Roxbury and interviewed an interracial couple. We thought this might be the perfect situation. The guy's name was Mel, and his girlfriend's (who we thought was his wife) name was Margaret Salinger. We called her Peggy or Peg because that's what she responded to. She is the daughter of J. D. Salinger, the author of *Catcher in the Rye*. After our interview, they accepted us into their five-bedroom estate. It was a beautiful home with a fitness center in the basement. Jasmine easily got another nursing job, while I had the same difficulty trying to find employment. Fortunately, within the second week, I found a position as Farm Director with Natick Youth and Human Resources.

This was a dream come true, though I didn't feel qualified. I had an academic background and farm experience, but the agency wanted someone to go the extra mile, work long hours, and make serious emotional commitments. In March 1979, I started working. This was an alternative farm for juvenile delinquents who were court-mandated to detention facilities. Our objective was to teach them life skills to deter further bad behavior. We tapped trees in the early morning for sap to make our own maple syrup. At lunch, we gathered slop from junior high schools to feed our sows. In the afternoon, we harvested and sold organic strawberries and asparagus to Whole Foods.

The hours of this job caused new problems in our relationship. I worked regular hours, 8 to 5. Peggy worked the night shift, 10:30 to 6:30 in the morning, and Mel and Jasmine worked the same swing shift, 3 to 10 p.m. While I tried to get to sleep after I picked Jasmine up at 10, she often decompressed and flirted with Mel in the kitchen. Though I asked her to come to bed, she frequently reneged to stay downstairs and talk with Mel, "My brother from another mother." This poem explains the complex entanglement.

If Peggy Had Been Home

If Peggy had been home,
I would have never stressed,
or tossed and turned to excess;
To get up to see if the kitchen light,
was partly on or dark like night,

If Peggy had been home,
I would have never stayed up
to view my wife with the lover's cup;
Listening to their delicious talk,
I had to watch her like a hawk;
If Peggy had been home,
she would've surely glammed,
and taken care of her lost lamb;

Taken care of his pimping walk,
His cool propensity to stalk;

If Peggy had been home,
he'd have been satisfied,
Because his love would be there by his side;
But Mel felt slighted and headed downstairs,
To play and caress my love's blonde hair;

Because Peg wasn't home, my spouse got played,
Got hooked by Peg's man and betrayed!
No matter how I tried, midnight oil burned bright,
Because Peg wasn't home to make it right;

If Peg had had a vision,
It could have kept me from collision;
My mind disengaged
As the drama played offstage,

Before taking the night shift, think,
Peggy broke the family link;
Life is hard when you feel alone,
Could it have been reversed,
If Peggy Was Home?

Chapter Fourteen

You Can Lead a Horse to Water...

"And be not conformed to this world: but be transformed by the renewing of your mind."
Romans 12:2a

It wasn't until a couple of months later, the first Saturday in June, that Jasmine and I talked about the midnight rendezvous. Over those two months, I processed my anger alone. I wanted to be sure my understanding of her infidelity was accurate. At that point, I could no longer keep quiet about what I suspected. She was sitting on the staircase, and I stood at the bottom, determined to explore the truth.

"You've been intimate with Mel!"

"Yes," she said softly.

"He's no good for you, and he's going to hurt you. It looks good now, but sooner or later, he's going to leave and rip you off." I gave her a fair warning about the scoundrel because I loved her.

Jasmine looked at me with surprising unconcern, as though she didn't care about her wayward fate.

I spoke with certainty about her affair and her destiny. Mel had told me the history of his playboy behavior during workouts in the fitness man cave. For six months, he had shared secrets during our weight-lifting sessions in the basement. He freely discussed his past escapades.

Mel joked, "You know, Rob, you have to work with what you're trying to catch. Use everything you have. Your charm, your smile, your time, and your body." He flexed his muscles on the mini-Nautilus machine.

"Is that how you got Peggy?"

"Yeah, she was just a wallflower, but she loved her some Mel," he smiled broadly. "You know how women love the chocolate. So, I used her interest and assets…"

"What assets?"

"You know Peggy won't divulge this, but she's the daughter of J.D. Salinger?

"You mean the author of *The Catcher in the Rye?*

"Yeah, and once I found that out, my eyes got big, and I knew she was my ticket to anywhere we wanted to go."

"And where has that been?"

"Man, we've been to New Hampshire, Maine, Nova Scotia, to places I would have never dreamed." He put his chest out with pride.

"Looks like you're getting your money's worth."

"Yeah, and I'm riding that pony to the bank!"

From Mel's stories about entrapping women, I realized he was a gold-digger. I had observed similar behavior with other males in college. Unfortunately, his smooth talk caught my wife's attention. His muscular physique, guitar-playing, and in-fectious smile had lured Jasmine into his web. Peggy seemed oblivious to Mel's womanizing, though her constant downward glance and soft-spoken demeanor indicated her spirit might be troubled. I wondered if, like other traumatized women, she was an accomplice to Mel's deception.

The primal impulse to physically fight him for Jasmine's affection entered my mind. But it wouldn't be a fair fight be-cause Mel had a black belt in Tae Kwon Do. Though I didn't possess the same physical strength, I had moral fiber. That char-acter strength was recorded and nurtured in my letters to my heart. In the genesis of our relationship, I said to Jasmine, "I can deal with anything except infidelity. If you play around on me with another guy while we're married, I'm gone." I was a man of my word, and it was time to get away from this toxic environment. It took one month after the staircase conversation with Jasmine for me to cut my losses. I prepared to depart from Boston with no desire to return. There was nothing left to say. Every time I looked at Jasmine that July, tears formed in the corners of my eyes. Crying should have relieved my pain. But I was so distraught that drenched handkerchiefs could not remove the pain in my heart.

After putting an advertisement in the *Boston Herald*, "Driver Needed," a woman named Katie responded. She agreed to be my travel buddy westward. On July 23rd, 1979, I bolted back to California in our white Honda Civic. Jasmine's infidelity with Mel had left me no choice. Her intimacy with this supposedly married man was the last straw.

As I departed on a hot, humid morning, my spirit was heavy. All the mistakes of the past year and my shattered marriage reverberated in my heart. What had gone wrong? Had anything gone right? What were the lessons to be learned?

For over two thousand miles, Katie and I took jabs, hitting at our imaginary punching bag. This short-bobbed, stout Caucasian woman from Utah was also emotionally wounded. She, too, was leaving a field of broken dreams for greener pastures.

Curious, I pondered out loud, "Why do people do what they do?"

Katie said, "I don't know. Just when you think you know someone, they fool you."

"Yeah, I was fooled. In fact, I was played. By two or possibly three con artists working together. I don't know, is life as bad as we think?"

"Possibly worse. What's great, though, is…to just be gone from that relationship. Good riddance!"

"Yeah, it's all in the past." But my heart hoped Jasmine would see the light and return to me.

We drove for 12 hours on the first day and felt good we had met our 500-mile goal. After a restful sleep in Motel-6, we continued processing our feelings with more sarcastic talk, trying to expunge the toxicity in our souls. Our conversation turned to satiric humor and animal metaphors.

"Katie, I hate to say it, but my wife acted like a pig the past few months. Jasmine was in the pig pen, but she liked the dirt and mud so much she kept going back."

"Yeah, you can lead a horse to water, but you can't make it drink."

"Sometimes, if the bird flies away, you just have to let it go."

"Yeah, but if it returns, you might think twice about flying with it again."

When Katie and I weren't exchanging jabs or proverbs, she slept while I reflected on the regrets of the past eighteen months. I had placed my desire to go back to seminary on hold. Though we discussed the idea in Kenya, Jasmine balked at my suggestion of attending seminary in 1978. I hated myself that I had always acquiesced to Jasmine's desires. This was part of a larger pattern of dashed hopes within the marriage. Now, it was time to set a personal plan for the future. It was my moment to assert myself as a single man again.

After another long day, Katie and I spent the second night in economy lodging, sharing a room. On the morning of the third day, I dropped Katie in Salt Lake City, Utah. I hugged and thanked her for the talks that kept our minds engaged as our hearts healed. Though the mileage marker read "San Francisco 735 miles," I could smell the California coastline. Four years of disc jockeying at UC Davis had filled my mind with memorable songs. Though my body was in Utah, lyrics from the

Golden State kept rolling in my head, like "California Dreamin'" by The Mamas & the Papas.

I arrived in Oakland and stayed with my parents for a week. They were happy I was back in California and completely supportive; they made it clear they would do whatever it took to help me be successful in the coming months. I talked with my older sister, Ronita, and her husband, Bill, about living together in Berkeley or North Oakland. After a week, we found a 2200 square foot house with two bedrooms, a front, and a backyard off 63rd Street. This would be my home for the next fourteen months.

Ronita, affectionately known as "Ro," was an admirable friend. Though she was six years my senior, Ro's support during my adolescent and young adult years helped me overcome shyness with women. She taught me how to dance and listened with empathy when relationship issues arose. One thing I needed after the breakup of my marriage was family support. From January to July 1979, life had been lonely on the East Coast. Ro provided that support as I restarted this new endeavor to get my life together. The major discussion and point of tension in our new living arrangement was the use of kitchen time. I was a vegetarian, and my housemates were carnivores. The smells and the kitchen space were challenging for two very different styles of cooking.

Ronita would often say, "What's all this green stuff in the sink?"

"I'm fixing a spinach salad, and I'll be cleaning collard greens."

"You need to eat some meat, and your cooking takes up a lot of space." Says who?

"Now, Ro, I have to stick to my diet to maintain discipline. You really ought to try it; you would feel better."

I was grateful that Ro provided a loving environment for change. Ro was the foundational rock that allowed me to find my voice. I could not have found my individual identity if I didn't have that unconditional base as the root of my transformation. She allowed me to express my individualism, which strengthened my self-discipline. The vegetarian lifestyle was a gift I took from my life with Jasmine. Changing my eating habits was healing and transformative. I continue to use that gift to maintain focus and purpose.

Chapter Fifteen

Believe in Yourself

"When then shall we then say to these things? If God be for us, who can be against us?"
Romans 8:31

I developed self-discipline in Kenya. This asset was the key to my strategic decisions. I tapped into this resource in every area of my growth. Amazingly, this time around, work prospects were plentiful and positive. Within two weeks, I had two interviews and got a job as a computer programmer at Pacific Gas and Electric (PG & E) headquarters in San Francisco. I traveled from Oakland to San Francisco daily, still gauging my energy and my happiness, wondering if this job was my long-term destiny.

I advanced up the ladder within PG & E, asking the big questions: "Was I happy? Could I see myself doing this job for the next thirty years? Would my passion for life and compassion for others be appreciated?" I waited for answers to these existential questions and turned my focus toward finding companionship.

I asked, "What do I want in a relationship?" I focused on dating African-American women. I thought over my personal history and experimented to see if my theories were correct. Could I communicate with a Black woman at a deep level? Could I have spontaneous fun and a spiritual relationship at the same time? Could we enjoy each other without the tug and pull of our respective family demands?

Christmas and New Year's Eve found me loved and adored by a precious woman of color named Beverly. She met my specifications in quiet ways. She was tall, 5-feet-8-inches, with shoulder-length African braids and beautiful mahogany skin. Her lips were full, her nose symmetrical, her eyes warm. For two months, I visited her at her home in San Francisco. Three times a week, we got together and talked. Beverly's calm demeanor brought solace to my soul. She made the 1979 holidays the most memorable in years. She attended my family's holiday gathering, and my aunt/godmother invited us later so she could become more acquainted. This was the only time in my history of bringing girlfriends home that she had done this. Her approval meant a lot.

Beverly stayed with a relative, Mattie, who attended Dad's church. I think word got out in the church community that I was available again. Beverly seemed like a match from heaven. The joy of visiting her involved simple, low-key fellowship in her bedroom. The nocturnal ambience was ideal for getting to know each other. When I walked into her love cave, she had arranged aromatic candles in bundles of three around the room. In the background, she played songs from Phyllis Hyman's album, "You Know How to Love Me" and "Sacred Kind of Love." We sat on the bed, and if Beverly suggested it, we lay down and embraced. Beverly wore glasses, but when the conversation became intimate, she removed them so we could have face time. Her quiet spirit was unlike any woman I had known. She was strong in character but willingly yielded in the subtle ways of love.

Just as I was feeling good about Beverly in particular and partnerships with Black women in general, Jasmine flew into town after New Year's 1980 for one last attempt at reconciliation, whatever that meant to her. We talked with greater honesty and transparency, but Jasmine was entangled in Mel's web of deception. Every time I brought up his name, Jasmine defended their union. It was a foregone conclusion they wanted to spend time together. They even had plans to move to Hawaii.

"So what's it going to be, Jasmine?"

"You know I love you, Robert, but it's time to move on. I will always love you, but we just can't seem to make each other happy anymore."

"Well, I've tried to do the best for you, but it seems like it's not enough. When you get hurt, remember what I said. I hope I'm around to comfort you when that happens."

Beverly dumped me the day after Jasmine's visit. She didn't want to compete with a separated wife, though I told her Jasmine and I were through. She didn't want her heart to go through the revolving door of marital separation and reconciliation. I understood her reasoning and didn't feel like fighting for her love. I learned once a woman makes up her mind, it is futile to change it. Beverly told me at the beginning that if we didn't make it, "she was through with men." It was her last chance at male/female bonding. I mourned for some time because I never got an opportunity to reconcile with her. A year later, when I saw Beverly walk down the aisle of an airplane I had boarded, she didn't even acknowledge my hello. I think she was still grieving our relationship.

Amid emotional challenges, I yearned for mental stimulation. In September 1979, I enrolled in courses leading to a Master's in business administration (MBA) at California State University, Hayward. Dad was a Black Studies instructor there, so I used the institution as a touchstone for family networking.

Dad had reached a new level of acceptance when he asked me to present a slideshow on "The Real Africa" to his class. This presentation was a rare opportunity to discuss the impact of Africa on America. Because Dad had visited Kenya, he elaborated on how Kenya had changed his perception of people, nature, and hardship. The exhilaration of storytelling on that occasion encouraged me to pursue graduate studies.

The first project in my MBA classes brought clarity to my academic pursuits. Since I worked for a public utility, I brought that experience to the classroom. I started the presentation by turning off the lights. Then, in the middle of the introduction, I said, "And God said let there be light," as I turned the switch on. The class and the teacher thought the presentation was creative. The illustration reignited the vows I had made in Kenya and York. Biblical language came naturally to me—one indicator of what still lay at the center of my heart.

In the next quarter, January 1980, I felt I needed to improve my writing skills, so I enrolled in "American Literature: Introduction in Poetry" at Alameda Junior College. This class changed my life. For the first time, I received personal tutelage from English professor Marlys Mayfield. She gave me extra books to read, one on critical thinking as well as poetry and fiction, and encouraged my creative presentations on the school's television station.

Marlys said, "Robert, you can do much more, just keep writing and believe in yourself."

I appreciated her mentorship and thanked her for her belief in me.

Marlys' faith in my ability to write and think critically gave me new confidence that ministry might be my chosen profession. I prayed, fasted, and sought God for two weeks about this decision. Finally, I made up my mind that ministry was my vocation. I told Dad, who was delighted.

In the spring of 1980, I felt the need to make good on the vow I had made to God during near-death experiences—the scorpion sting of 1975, the high fever with malaria in 1976, and the "I'm going to kill you" incident in 1977. Since the speech impediment issues were resolved and I had begun writing proficiently, I was ready for ministry.

But I wasn't ready for Dad's medical diagnosis. Three months earlier, I had been sitting with Dad in my parents' kitchen when I saw Dad's thumb twitch.

I asked, "What's going on?"

He could barely speak. "I'm, I'm…having a tremor," he muttered as I watched the twitch intensify.

I looked on helplessly as the tremor violently took him to his knees, then to his side as he rolled into the living room, kicking the floor.

"Mom, come quick! Dad's having a seizure!"

Finally, after ten minutes, the convulsions stopped, and we propped Dad up before taking him to bed.

One week after the seizure, diagnostic imaging revealed Dad had a brain tumor called "astrocytoma." The brain surgeons needed to operate immediately. Surgery was scheduled for the Monday after Easter, 1980. We hoped the afterglow of Resurrection Sunday would affect the surgery results. Unfortunately, the doctors reported after surgery that what they thought was Stage 3 was actually Stage 4. The family prepared for the worst. We wondered how much time Dad had left. Every day became more precious because any day could be Dad's last.

The lost opportunities to be with Dad, to know him better, filled my heart with regret. Life could have been different if only I had followed my heart. If I hadn't gotten married but had traveled directly home to pursue ministry. I beat myself up thinking of the eighteen months we could have worked together. My heart filled with grief that I had not received my call to ministry earlier. So, my call to ministry was bitter-sweet, yet I learned that all things happen for a reason and in due season. Time taught me the wisdom even of grief as I held this sacred cup of understanding.

Chapter Sixteen

Facing Giants with Faith

"For I am not ashamed of the gospel of Christ, for it is the power of God unto salvation for everyone who believes."
Romans 1:16a

Everyone in the family rallied around Dad's struggle with cancer. The terminal disease had been part of our family story for generations. Grandma Mary Lou, Mom's mother, died from colon cancer when I was three months old. Grandpa Bud, Dad's father, died from throat cancer when I was six. The vision of Bud's body lying in state for three days in my grandparents' living room was unforgettable. I thought the dead were supposed to reside at funeral homes, not in rooms adjacent to our sleeping quarters. His cold, lifeless shell left an impression on my psyche. I learned life was like a vapor that appears for a little time and vanishes away. I had a memorable visual because death might be a few feet away, so I wanted to live each sacred second with full appreciation.

That awareness was reawakened as I kept vigil with Dad. Mom's work as a high school counselor required mental concentration. She was relieved when one of her three children took their turn as caretaker. I relished this quality time with Dad. His busy life as a pastor, adjunct professor, and community organizer had left a few hours for father-son bonding. My duty was more than a chore; it was the first phase of anticipatory grief and spiritual growth.

I arrived after sunset and slowly walked to the master bedroom. Mindful of Dad's sensitive ears, I tip-toed towards his bed and spoke softly. "Hi, Dad, how's it going this evening?"

His gold tooth peeked out from a painful smile. Dad reached out with the arm closest to his heart. I met his gesture with my left arm. We grabbed each other's triceps like two Roman soldiers after a long battle. I kissed his bald forehead and embraced his broad shoulders.

"Thank you, son; I've waited to see you all day. Now I can get some rest."

"Thanks, Dad, for your love and prayers. I know I wouldn't be where I am today without you."

"I may not show it, son, but you know I'm excited about your next move in ministry."

Whatever duties I took on during the next nine hours of the vigil were worth all the love expressed in those few moments of dialogue. We had waited a lifetime to connect but always missed the opportunity to open the "letters of our hearts." I lay down on the floor with peace, knowing Dad was only a few feet away.

As I slept, Jonah's narratives entered my dreams. Like Jonah, I was the reluctant prophet. Since childhood, I had felt God calling me to ministry. Honestly, I had no idea what that meant, but I knew at an early age I was a spiritual being. My developmental deficiencies prevented me from thinking I could be used by God. I spoke to God with audible excuses: "I can't talk, I can't do what Dad does, I can't write, how can you use me?" All these excuses made me reluctant to pursue ministry. Ironically, these very excuses became my stepping stones to deliverance.

The speaking deficiency was resolved after four years of being a DJ on UC Davis radio and two years of teaching in Kenya.

Now, in Dad's presence, I was about to resolve the writing deficiency. I waited for dawn to receive lessons from this orator and first-class preacher.

Upon rising, I fixed Dad's breakfast. As I prepared the food, I periodically checked on his morning maneuvers. To minimize movement up and down the stairs, I took his breakfast to him on a tray. I hoped Dad would eat more that day than yesterday, but I understood chemo-radiation caused nausea. He slept for an hour to help his food digest.

When he awoke, he was in a talkative mood. So, we discussed the message I was preparing to preach on June 22nd, 1980. Since this was my first sermon, preparation was basic. I had not started seminary, so I had no homiletical principles to rely on.

Dad asked, "What is your text?"

"1 Samuel 17: 45-51, where David kills Goliath."

"And what's your title?"

"Facing Giants with Faith!"

"What profound pearls of wisdom are you going to convey to the congregation that they have never heard before?"

"I'm going to share how David's story relates to my story."

"You've got to go further than that, son. You've got to empower people through stories and tell them how this biblical text is going to help them live the Christian life. Encourage them in loving, faithful, prayerful ways."

For over an hour, Dad grilled me and prompted me until I had nothing left to suggest. "Now, you're ready to start your sermon."

Though it was a difficult process, this was my first lesson in sermon preparation. Though Dad rejected all my suggestions and outlines, I accepted his loving feedback and critique.

In the weeks before I was to preach, I honed the thoughts Dad considered relevant. I retyped, prayed, and revisited this sermon several times before handing the final copy to Dad on

June 20th. When June 22nd finally came, I was both relieved and excited. Dad made several hundred copies of my sermon.

During the message at the Church of All Faiths, the entire congregation sat on the edge of their seats, encouraging me to speak a word into their life. In the Black church tradition, if the preacher speaks a word that touches their hearts, the congregants audibly respond with words of encouragement like, "Amen," "Hallelujah," or "Preach, Son. "I preached with passion, talking about all the giants I had faced. I spoke of my speech impediment, scorpion sting, and failed marriage. I concluded my sermon with: "It doesn't matter what the giants look like; God will give you smooth stones to overcome them."

Dad treated my first sermon as a historic event. He even asked for donations for the manuscript as people were leaving. That was the only time I saw a sermon sold after service.

My decision to go into ministry had transformed Dad's previous view of me. When I was in college, Dad had no understanding of my vocational direction. I remember Dad's harsh words to Mom from years before: "If Robert can't do anything else, he can always be a pimp." I never asked Dad why he spoke those words, but I did not sense he was simply using "reverse psychology." During those undergrad years, my parents were unapproachable and lacked understanding of matters of my heart.

Now, five years later, my acceptance to San Francisco Theological Seminary changed Dad's perceptions. I used his negative judgment as a driving force. I aspired to be the epitome of a pastoral and spiritual caregiver. This path was a calling from the throne room, and I pursued it to honor God's grace.

The following month, in July, I preached on the second Sunday, but it was different. Lethargy diminished Dad's excitement. After service, I stood in front of the altar, receiving accolades from church members. Mother Jenkins, an eighty-year-old member, stepped up and embraced me. After her firm hug, she immediately fell to the floor. As I saw liquid leave her body, wetting the carpet, I sensed she had died. Someone called 911, and ten minutes later, the paramedics confirmed her death.

Seeing a person die was shocking, but it was another lesson that reaffirmed life is like a vapor. Anything is possible at any time. This was the last time I shared the pulpit with Dad. For political reasons, the interim pastor, Rev. Snell, kept me away from the pulpit. It was the last time I would preach at this church for a year.

I was glad my earthly mentor was still alive that day. Though he was weak, I had gleaned everything from his treasure chest. Dad had preached the Word since 1952. During that span, his real-life experiences were relevant. He used his military background and his many experiences of vicious racial discrimination as touchstones of resilience. The congregations he spoke to resonated with his sermons.

During August, a period of temporary remission, we traveled together to the International Council of Community Churches (ICCC) in San Antonio, Texas. Dad had recently been elected President of ICCC. He planned to give the Plenary Address on the first night of the Conference. This was the umbrella organization for the church Dad had co-founded in 1965, the Church of All Faiths. Dad was blessed with parliamentary wisdom and the preaching gift that brought this international and interracial group together. After we arrived, Dad thought he might be strong enough to deliver his speech. But that night, he weakened and called me to his room.

"Son, you know how much this speech means to me…been involved in ICCC for 15 years."

"Yes, I understand."

"I would love to deliver this address, but I am afraid I won't be able to do it justice. Do you think you could give the speech?"

I knew I had to step up. "Sure, whatever you need, Dad."

"Well, we need to go over it line by line."

Dad rested for an hour as I ate dinner. When he awoke, we prepped. Dad discussed the intent of this message and the key points about Christian unity, justice, and reconciliation. We stayed with it all Sunday evening and Monday morning until I was ready to deliver the speech to him at noon.

I felt empowered when I got up before the crowd in the Convention Hall Monday night. The moment felt as if I had practiced all my life for "such a time as this." As I looked at the 500 delegates from 150 churches, I felt welcomed. They gave me kudos for my courage and accolades for my presentation. This was a confidence builder as I prepared for seminary.

Since my time in Africa, I was determined to start my career before I reached twenty-seven years old. I was resolved to change my earthly father's negative perception, following my heavenly father's guidance. Prayerfully, I hoped to function at the same level of intelligence I had shown in elementary school, where I was voted "The smartest 6th grader." I believed I was operating in my gifts. I knew that through the process, God would make "the crooked places straight and the rough places smooth."

Chapter Seventeen

What Would Jesus Do?

"And we know that all things work together for good to those who love God."
Romans 8:28a

I considered the challenges of graduate school, hoping I could function with cognitive excellence. Having been distracted as an undergraduate at UC Davis by three jobs and a trio of crazy roommates, I knew my best was yet to come. During my academic hiatus after college, I read about the differences between the hemispheres of the dual brain. I wanted to develop both left-brain organization and right-brain creativity. In preparation for Biblical Hebrew, I took a class at Hillel House, Berkeley. I learned the twenty-two letters of the Hebrew alphabet, with their odd guttural sounds and diacritical markings. This intensive learning caused optic nerve strain, eventually requiring reading glasses. Unexpectedly, the Hebrew instructors at the seminary were irritated when, coming in with the good instruction from Hillel, I pointed out their diacritical errors. I realized there is more to life than being right: having peaceful relationships is more important.

Living in Marin County, a quiet place full of natural beauty, helped me realize how inner peace maximizes learning. I lived in the butlers' quarters, which helped me stay humble in preparation for ministry. After living with no running water or electricity in Kenya, these accommodations made this place a palace. The only obligation was working one day a week for rent. The town of Ross was filled with tree-covered hills, winding creeks, and landscaped streets. The best feature of the property was the creek that ran through it and the views of Mt. Tamalpais in the distance.

The tragic moments of that first year of the seminary were the days leading to Dad's death. I made frequent trips across the bay to see him between classes and work. In the last few months before his demise in March 1981, he was placed in Hospice Care. The family members embraced this news with different stages of denial, shock, and anticipatory grief.

On the night of Dad's earthly departure, I got to the hospital in the nick of time. That evening, I attended a lecture in Berkeley with a classmate. Knowing Dad's condition, I prayed he would still be alive when we arrived. After the lecture ended, we drove to Kaiser Hospital in Hayward. We knew the death angel was near because the family was gathered around the bed. Skin and body changes made the room smell like nail polish remover. Everybody said, "Dad's waiting for you." When I put my hand on his shoulder, I could feel his labored breathing. I led the family in a word of prayer, thanking God for Dad's life and this loving community. Two minutes after the prayer, my fifty-eight-year-old Dad breathed his final breath.

During those last seven months of Dad's life, my dating life was chaotic. I cut ties with Becky, a legal secretary I had dated since January. Margaret, a Ph.D. candidate I had known since high school, had excellent spousal potential except for her one liability: she hated God. Maintaining healthy alliances seemed important as I explored potential life partners. "He who finds a wife finds a good thing. And obtains favor from the Lord" (Pro. 18:22). I knew I could not begin life as a pastor, single.

On April 1st, 1981, my grieving was compounded with physical brokenness. As you recall, it was on this sunny Friday morning that I was tasked with painting the owner's master bedroom on the second floor. With a brush in one hand and a paint can in the other, I painted the wooden slats from the entrance of the room to the outer door. The combination of the second-floor heat and paint fumes was a toxic cocktail. The fumes were disorienting and caused me to paint myself into that corner on the balcony. On the balcony, I looked for a moment at the weeping willow branches and listened to the rushing brook below. As I gazed at Mt. Tamalpais in the distance, I placed my left hand on the balcony rail twenty feet above the driveway, leaned, and the rail broke, sending my 180-pound body in a downward descent to the cobblestones below.

As I wrote earlier, I was out like a rock, and only God knows how long I stayed motionless on the ground. It felt like an eternity. I gradually awakened to find my fate—I was alive. I checked my hands and feet to see if I could move. I felt blood on my face and pain in every bone of my body. Slowly, I got up one foot in front of the other and walked 100 feet to view the damage in the mirror. I was horrified by the sight. Blood covered the image of my forehead, nose, and cheekbones. I barely saw my face as I wiped the thick red liquid from my eyes.

Ms. Smith, the 70-year-old widow of the house, left her car and walked down the driveway toward my flat. A red fire truck appeared at the house within minutes to take me to Ross Hospital. After I arrived at the Emergency Room, the nurse took me into a private room to stitch up my forehead. As she put in each of the twelve sutures, I pondered my future.

I reflected on my fractured life. If I had broken any bones, my commitment to do tasks one day a week would be impossible. If I couldn't work, our rental agreement would be broken. Usually, Ms. Smith and I didn't talk during the week except about chores. I wondered, where would I live? My whole world crashed with this "fall from grace." I lifted these petitions to the only One who could resolve the problem. I wanted and needed a way out of this mess.

X-ray results confirmed a broken left wrist, sprained ligaments on the right knee, and a large gash on my right forehead. As the fire truck dropped me off at home, I became melancholy. I basked in the shade of the forty-foot pine, still able to appreciate the view of Mt. Tamalpais—maybe for one last time. One week later, the widow gave me notice: Move out by May 1st.

The answer to my prayer came from the San Francisco Theological Seminary (SFTS) housing office. They told me in person, "There's one apartment on Le Conte, Berkeley, on the third floor."

"I'll take it," I said as I went whistling out of the office with an attitude of gratitude. My living space increased with this new move. My bedroom was larger than the entire flat in Ross. I wondered if Dad was my guardian angel in this transition.

In honor of the blessing, I put scriptural declarations all over the walls of the kitchen and living room. I had learned the power of visualization, and these walls encouraged ongoing theological reflection. Before the saying was powerful in the 1990s, I put "What Would Jesus Do?" in black twelve-inch press-on alphabets in my living room. In my kitchen, I put Jesus' challenging words, "O ye of little faith" (Matthew 6:30). In my bedroom, sleep had its own wisdom that said, "Come unto me all ye that are heavy-laden, and I will give thee rest" (Matthew 11:28). These affirmations motivated me when thoughts and creativity waned.

The summer of 1981 was calm and peaceful. It was a respite from caring for Dad and providing encouraging words to my mom. I was tired of people assuming I was the care provider for the whole world. I asked, where is my support? Where is that someone I can lean on when I get exhausted and weary of giving support to others?

I found my support in a Black seminarian named Estee. Somewhere in my mental and spiritual imagination, she seemed like the perfect fit, but I was discreet. Entering theology school, I learned to be cautious about the true intentions of women in seminary. I was on high alert. Were they in school for the purpose of ministry or finding a mate? I lowered my prejudices in the presence of Estee.

Estee and I met on the second Friday afternoon in January 1981 in the Christian Fellowship building on the SFTS campus. When I walked into the backroom, Estee appeared to be acting out a pantomime for children. I stood against the wall as she entertained the children with dance, swift turns, and animation. I said in my mind, "This girl's got a lot of energy." She was a slender five-foot-five-inches with a face like Diana Ross and the youthful look of an undergrad. In the back of my mind, Estee seemed like a new incarnation of my first love, Yvette. As Estee finished dancing, I spoke up: "Hi, I'm Robert. Who are you?"

Chapter Eighteen

Everything's in the Backseat

*"What then shall we say to these things? If God be for us,
who can be against us?"*
Romans 8:28

After I introduced myself to the dancing Black angel, she held out her hand as though she were Cinderella waiting for a kiss. I grasped her right hand and placed my left hand gently on top to calm her beating heart.

"I'm Estee, just having fun with these kids. Isn't it exciting to share the Gospel in creative ways? I just love it, love it!"

Estee's enthusiasm was intoxicating. I just wanted to fan the flame of her joy, but I said, "Are you in school here, living on campus?"

"I just got here a few days ago. I'm house-sitting for a woman in San Anselmo until I get a permanent apartment here. Well, what's your class schedule so I can see you again?"

"I've got New Testament on Monday morning. We'll try after that."

"Okay, see you in the Chapel after class." I started to leave, then paused. "Do you have a phone number?"

"Yes." I handed Estee a pen, and she scribbled her phone number on my work schedule. "Any time before 9 p.m."

All weekend, I wanted to call but didn't want to seem desperate. Nothing is worse than pursuing a woman with your tongue out. I played it cool and waited. Though I distrusted my own impulsiveness, I found Estee's constant attention supernaturally nurturing. She was comfortable as she reached to touch my arm and gazed into my needy soul.

This woman was appealing. I knew if we continued, fireworks were about to erupt. After three months, we dated around the 1981 Christmas holidays. After New Year's, we flew to Estee's home in Los Angeles, picked up her car, and took a beautiful road trip back. She had Diana Ross's lips and facial structure. I wanted to know more about this spirit-filled Presbyterian who acted Pentecostal. I hoped I would meet her mother's approval.

We flew into LAX. We picked up Estee's car from her place on a Saturday. The next day, we went to a house worship in Compton. There was an anointing on this service I had never experienced. As the service started, the house worshippers talked about receiving the Holy Spirit. Several members asked me if I wanted to "receive the baptism of the Holy Spirit." As they prayed and laid hands on me, I began to speak with a language my lips had never uttered. The supernatural power of this prayer dropped me to my knees, and I continued to praise God. I must have knelt for over twenty minutes speaking with words I could not understand. It was like "rivers of living waters" flowing through my inner self. After the service, Estee smiled because she knew we had reached a new level in our relationship.

The following day, I met Mary, Estee's mother. It was the most uncomfortable initial meeting with a girlfriend's parent I'd ever experienced. From the beginning to the end of our two-hour conversation, her questions were intense. Her inquiries felt like an inquisition. Estee, at that point, was no help. She was MIA in the kitchen, leaving me to my own devices and, I suppose, trusting me to manage this interview in my own way. She asked me about my parents' background, their schooling, jobs, and places we had lived. I thought answering these questions would lead to final approval, but it did not. The inquiry only made me uneasy about having Mary as a potential mother-in-law. She was the worst cheerleader for her daughter's happiness.

Now I understood Estee's warning about her mother's aggressive way of getting to know people. Mary's psychoanalysis made me feel violated. She removed the emotional clothing of my life without touching one piece of garment. I never sat in the hot seat of Mary's living room again. I whispered to Estee, "I'm ready to leave." She already had car keys in hand, a sweater on her shoulders, and the look of departure in her eyes. I shook Mary's hand, and Estee just waved goodbye to her mother. As we drove to the next engagement, the atmosphere inside the car was quiet. The radio was off, but the brain waves were loud.

I said, "I understand now why you left home. Your mom's intrusiveness drove you away."

"Yeah, it's been a rough road dealing with emotional abuse. She drives people away with all her questions. I tell her to cease and desist, but she's stuck in a pattern and won't listen."

"Thank you for finally rescuing me from the interrogation, and forgive me if my armpits are on fire; I was sweating bullets back there."

"I've got a white towel in the backseat if you can find it."

"Yeah, you seem to have everything in the backseat."

"It may not be organized, but if you dig deep enough, you'll find what you need."

Traveling back to Northern California from LA, we listened to our favorite music. Songs like "When Love Comes Calling" and "Sun Goddess" filled Estee's Toyota sedan. She loved to dance, and when we needed a road break, we'd pull over at a rest stop and prance around the car. Estee's spontaneity offered a sharp contrast to my structured way of living. I had impulsive tendencies, but spontaneity had gotten me in trouble. I spoke when I should be quiet and stayed silent when I should emote. During Estee's nurturing, awareness and wisdom came quickly. I learned to respond to her emotional cues in hopes of preventing the mistakes of the past. I loved Estee. She understood my complaints about the established religion and still encouraged an intimate walk with God.

My fondness for her increased exponentially with every word shared and kiss exchanged. She was spontaneous even when we were alone in her apartment or mine. I never rushed our times of intimacy. I just tried to reciprocate every advance with a response. Kisses on the lips turned into smooches on the face, arms, and fingers. She treated every moment of intimacy with excitement as if it were the first time. Her eyes lit up, and she bounced in front of me as if she was getting ready to open a Christmas present. We never talked about safe sex or the possibility of Estee getting pregnant. I didn't even know if she was able to have children. We cared for each other and reveled in our physical closeness. We used our intimate times the way people use coffee breaks. Intimacy was our energy stimulant. We used it to start a paper and resolve ideas when we got stuck. Her love, our love, was filled with promise for the present and hope for the future.

Two months after we returned from Los Angeles, I applied for a ministerial internship in Oakland. Without any effort, a six-month job manifested. Dad's death should have created an opportunity at the Church of All Faiths, but it was not a good fit. Pastor Snell was threatened by my preaching and presence. So, I was doubly glad the internship with Amos Temple CME Church in Oakland materialized.

March 1982 brought pivotal discussions. Should I fully pursue a CME calling or some other denomination? What was the best path to a pastoral assignment? I needed a job. I had serious romantic thoughts about Estee. The more we spent time together, the more I thought she was my intended wife. But we were tired of shifting study locations between Estee's apartment in Marin and mine in Berkeley. It was time to come together. Two weeks later, I asked Estee to marry me.

We created special invitations with a silhouetted view of our faces surrounded by a heart. We planned every detail of the wedding. All the planning was going smoothly until an old habit resurfaced. Estee had a clutter problem, and it made my organized mind ballistic. Piles of papers in her car and house troubled my spirit. I wanted to show compassion, but I had developed an obsessive-compulsive disorder over her disorganization. I told Estee in a fit of frustration, "If you cannot keep a car or room clean, how are you going to take care of a house or children?" Her clutter was too much for me to comprehend, but those impulsive words haunted me in the coming months.

Chapter Nineteen

Walk Around Seven Times

"The Spirit of the Lord God is upon Me because the Lord has anointed Me to preach good news to the poor; He has sent Me to heal the broken hearted, to proclaim liberty to the captives."
Isaiah 61:1a

I didn't want Estee to leave, but the clutter issues could not be resolved by talking. Internally, I had other stressors that I had never discussed. I feared getting married to her without having a job. I didn't have money to buy a ring, pay for a wedding, or even go on a honeymoon. I had preconceived ideas about how marriage should commence. Without those pieces in place, I felt I wouldn't be giving our marriage a fair start. We discussed the possibility of getting together later if I got a job. Within a few days of my outburst about clutter, Estee packed up her things, got in her cluttered car, and traveled back to Los Angeles.

While my relationship with Estee suffered, I redirected my energy towards theological training. 1982 was the beginning of my internship. East Oakland provided excellent opportunities to utilize my gifts in an urban setting. I found a user-friendly situation with the senior pastor of Amos Temple CME church, Rev. John Borens. My first encounter with John was in 1960 when he had been stationed at Barksdale AFB near Shreveport,

LA. Dad pastored the lead CME church in Shreveport, and Airman Borens visited our fellowship frequently. As a special favor, John was invited to join our family meals at the parsonage. He started receiving mentoring from Dad—mentoring I would have cherished—as he considered ministry. Almost twenty years later, Rev. Borens reciprocated Dad's kindness by accepting me.

Rev. Borens gave me opportunities to serve in critical aspects of ministry. For six months, I preached, taught, and served on committees not usually assigned to interns to support the development of Amos Temple. Rev. Borens pushed me as if I were the pastor. My internship ended in September 1982, and I prepared to return to a regular class schedule feeling ready and eager to move on into ministry.

During September's Northern California Annual Conference, I became an ordained elder on Wednesday. Two days later, Bishop E.E. Cummings appointed me Pastor-in-Charge of St. Stephen CME in Fairfield, CA. September 2nd, 1982, was the happiest day of my ministerial career. I had one year to complete seminary, but it didn't matter because I was gainfully employed. While my classmates wondered about interviews and passing boards, I focused on finishing my final academic year as I found my now-secure footing in a new congregation. Miraculously, I was in the job I had prayed for since I was five years old. God had restored me despite speech impediments, writing challenges, reluctance, and even occasional resistance to entering ministry. All the crucibles seemed worth the struggle. I tried to notify Estee in Los Angeles, but we didn't connect. On the same day I was ordained an elder, I met an ordained deacon named Lawanda. Lawanda was not my usual type of woman to befriend, but the spiritual euphoria of the moment made this meeting a unique experience.

On the night of my appointment, I drove to St. Stephen's and prayed in the parking lot. I asked God, "What should I do to thank You for this opportunity?" God said, "Walk around the church seven times." So, I went to my Bible and reviewed the passages about how Joshua got the victory against Jericho. In the dark, by faith, I walked around the church seven times, binding and tearing down strongholds that had been established at the church. I asked God to lose a spirit of deliverance and praise over any person who entered the doors of St. Stephen.

The St. Stephen's congregation was receptive to my ministerial endeavors. This church had had only one previous pastor, the founder Joe Davis. Rev. Davis was a man in his sixties, and I was not yet thirty. I brought a level of energy to a congregation that was primed for church growth. The most novel program I started was the Evangelistic Committee. In November 1982, I did a two-week evangelism preaching series on Sundays, followed by Bible study on Wednesdays. Eight people signed up to be on the Evangelistic Team. We used the information from Visitors' Guest cards to create our visitation list. After prayer on the first night, we went to the home of a mother and daughter who had expressed interest. Four of the team members went into a house where we thought the two of them were living. Within thirty minutes, several people emerged from their bedrooms and joined us in the living room for prayer. Eleven people in that home confessed Jesus as their personal Savior. What a powerful confirmation from the Lord! We encouraged them to come to the church. That Sunday, they joined. By the end of the first week, we had received fifty commitments from homes we had visited.

This church also gave me an opportunity to explore prison ministry. One new member had a husband in the California Men's Facility, ten miles from the church, and we visited him. I thought the visitation was cordial but found out later that the inmate balked at the idea that I had driven his wife to see him. There are some dimensions of ministry you can't teach; you just must experience the tension. As it turned out, I couldn't continue bringing her to see him, but I believed God would make a way to pursue prison ministry at a later season.

Though the church's ministry was thriving, my self-care was at an all-time low. I missed and needed a touch from a help-mate. I yearned for the spontaneity I had grown accustomed to. That feeling caused me to think about looking for a wife once again.

I wrote a small list of qualities that I expected in a wife. I wanted someone who loved the Lord. Someone who loved being my wife and encouraged me with prayer and intercession. I wanted someone who was emotionally mature. I didn't have time to play emotional games with people. I needed someone who was balanced, honest, secure, and genuine. I wanted someone who inspired me to do more in the context of a strong mutual bond. I wanted a helpmate who had experienced the power of God in her life and knew how to pray for deliverance for others. I wanted a friend who enjoyed being with me and wanted to be the mother of our children.

I thought Lawanda was a prospect until I saw her atypical tendencies. On Saturday nights, when I was putting the finishing touches on my sermon, she would have an angina attack. Her heart condition recurrently needed emergent medical attention. I thought it was unusual that the attacks always happened on Saturday evening around 7 p.m. After going to the hospital, the doctors would resolve the issue, but Lawanda always stole an expensive thermometer. After this happened a few times, I had concerns. Those criminal tendencies became more apparent when Lawanda and I were driving in Los Angeles one weekend. After a sharp left turn, she got pulled over by the LA Police. The next thing I knew, Lawanda was in handcuffs by the right rear wheel. Sheriffs eventually took her to Sybil Brand County Jail, where I spent the weekend getting money to bail her out. Her record of petty theft showed up. I got her released, but I knew my time with her was limited.

My antenna went up as I began to observe people God brought into my environment. Church members invited me to dinner, and a friend of theirs, an available woman, would show up, too. Women I didn't know started attending church and sat in the front row while I preached. They wore short skirts to bring attention to themselves from me or the large percentage of men in our congregation. As a single pastor, I felt their risqué apparel was intended for my eyes. Some of the male ushers would talk about this phenomenon before church. I had a meeting with the Usher Board and asked them to redirect all short skirts to an area away from the front row. We even bought extra-large cloth covers to place over parishioners in case they "fell out"—when the Spirit touched them and they fell on the floor.

As I continued to get dinner invitations, I read articles about the Black preacher's emotional and psychological impact on women congregants. The research revealed some women fantasized about preachers during the sermon. This phenomenon appeared to happen more in the Black church because the male Black preacher historically held a powerful position of authority in the community. Understanding some of these subtleties changed how I did pastoral counseling. I had to be careful about hugging women. I had to be mindful about being in my office with a woman alone or alone in the church with a woman. I understood why two older women always accompanied me when I made pastoral visits. I learned that perception is everything. There are lines a pastor should not cross.

Chapter Twenty

Here We Go Again

*"A bishop then must be blameless, the husband of one wife,
temperate, sober-minded, of good behavior, hospitable, able
to teach."*
1 Timothy 3:2

In December 1982, I received an invitation to attend a February Food Bank meeting for Paraclete County. Every move I made these days passed through the sieve of my heart and the operating module of my mind. I took it all into prayer. Three times a week, I gathered with anyone who wanted to come to church early to pray before the workday began. As a pastor, I was busy with Advent services and placed the Food Bank invitation in the pending tray. I needed some discernment about participating in another community commitment. I had six months to complete my Master of Divinity degree, and I didn't want to get overextended. I wanted to end my seminary days on a positive note.

The number of hungry, homeless people I saw daily in Fairfield prompted my interest in the Food Bank. They had been there for a long time, but now I began to see them in a new way. I felt compelled to respond to Jesus' message in Matthew 25:35: "For I was hungry, and you gave Me food, I was thirsty, and you gave Me drink; I was a stranger, and you took Me in." So, one day in the first months of my pastorate, I prayerfully picked up a homeless fellow. I took him home with me and al-lowed him to take a shower. I gave him a pair of shoes, socks, pants, a shirt, and a warm jacket. I made a meal for him and later dropped him off at a place where he felt comfortable. He didn't say much beyond simple thanks when I dropped him off. But it was obvious I had been called to meet this need that day, and I was glad to obey. That experience prompted me to call the Food Bank and tell them the day before the meeting, "I'll be in attendance." After the gathering, I met the director, Angel Speaks. She was friendly and hard-working, but I didn't have any "love at first sight" attraction.

A few weeks after our initial meeting, Angel started coming to St. Stephen to hear me preach. I noticed her, especially dur-ing the offertory, in her gold sweater and long paisley skirt. She sashayed along the aisles with her black boots and short-cropped hair. Compared to the other women, she appeared con-servative, humble, and inconspicuous. Angel didn't seem to be the type of woman who was looking to attract a preacher. Of course, clothes don't always express the ulterior desires of the heart, but I learned they were a valuable indicator of intentions.

From March to July 1983, Angel and I were often involved in one another's church functions. Often, I visited her congre-gation in Benicia, Church of Anointing (COA), hoping to un-derstand her upbringing. Like protective parents, Angel's lead-ership wanted to ensure I was the right kind of man for her. I met Pastor Mercy, and she allowed me to preach and pray for the congregation. Between ministry at St. Stephen's and COA, getting to know the real Angel was challenging. In our spare time, I took on intimate responsibilities of caring for and bond-ing with Alecia, Angel's eighteen-month-old daughter. Without instruction, I quickly learned how to be a father to a child that I didn't know and couldn't verbally communicate with. In the last week of July, I thought, "Here we go again," and proposed to Angel. She said, "Yes."

With this proposal, we terminated all other relationships that might divert our attention from our pending marriage. I called Los Angeles and cut off a two-month long-distance liaison with Laghretta "Summa Cum" Bell, a graduate of UCLA. Laghretta and I had spent months talking about preaching, teaching, and the demands of ministry. She also had a child, but that hadn't been a deterrent since I felt experienced after precious time with young Alecia. With her 5-foot-10-inch stature, she challenged me to a game of basketball. I loved the banter between us.

She said, "You think you can guard me."

"I am going to stick to you like glue."

"Watch out, stick too close, and you might get hurt."

"I'll take my chances and let you kiss my bruises."

Laghretta was brilliant. She had extensive church experience, spiritual wisdom, and beauty. She even attended my graduation in May 1983. Unfortunately, the physical distance of 360 miles made face-to-face dialogue difficult. I was saddened to say goodbye to this Black diamond, but it was time.

I also traveled to San Francisco to speak with Mariam Rose, my longtime acquaintance from UC Davis. After the Dear John letter from Yvette, I had taken an eight-month hiatus from dating to manage the college radio station, KDVS. At the time, I felt navigating my senior year and supervising the radio staff needed my unequivocal attention. Mariam was a sultry-voiced disc jockey who melted my heart every time she spoke. She gave me the courage to re-enter the dating world.

Mariam was also an excellent writer who challenged my own creative expression. After I joined the Peace Corps in August 1975, Mariam and I wrote for six months. I'm not sure what caused the impasse, but the letters just stopped coming. Later, in July 1979, when I had separated from my first wife and returned to California, Mariam was there to console me. Over the years, she had become a consummate companion. But whenever I discussed marriage, there was hesitation about religious involvement. She didn't want to be a pastor's wife. Once again, I loved someone—Mariam—who didn't understand my spiritual passion. Her resistance eliminated her as a long-term mate.

We met on Friday afternoon at her oceanfront condo. We enjoyed our leisurely walk along the beach, heading to the Chinese Tea Garden. Mariam told me about her gallery work and Tai Chi classes, and I talked about the church. We walked over the Tea Garden bridge, and I took pictures of the lake, Mariam, and the Buddha statue. After appreciating these vistas, we sat on the bench, and I told her we had to stop seeing each other.

She asked, "Why?" I said, "Because I'm getting married." There was sadness on her face as tears filled our eyes. Silence came over us like a dark cloud before the rain. This separation was particularly hard because Mariam and I did have emotional equity. For the past eight years, we had exchanged letters, prayers, and mutual support. This abrupt closure felt like death. I wished I had found similar emotional equity with Angel—moments of laughter and dancing, fixing dinner and walks to the park—not just "church time." But the pastor in me felt an urgency to get married.

For the next six months, Angel and I were on an unstoppable train leading to marriage. Each day brought increased affection and desire for the future. Spiritual interest had always excited my interest, and Angel's commitment to God enhanced her attraction. Her devotion to the Word and effortless ability to use scripture secured her position. Her ability to cook and her work ethic made me feel Angel was the one. She met the criteria. The early stages of care with Alecia made me feel confident I could be a good husband and father. On the surface, the platform was set for an effective and successful ministry. I never questioned if my urgency to get married may have blinded my in-depth assessment.

But I asked myself on many occasions, "Do I really know how Angel feels?" I wondered about her relationship with Mr. G.—Alecia's father. I asked Angel about previous relationships, and I believed her responses. But still, I was apprehensive about her level of honesty. Unfortunately, Angel and I hadn't spent much casual time together and hadn't developed the deep trust we both hoped for.

With these concerns, we married at my father's church, Church of All Faiths, Oakland, on Jan. 21st, 1984. The wedding had 300 guests, six bridesmaids and ushers, and a reception in the fellowship hall. We honeymooned near the Berkeley Marina and tried to embrace our love. By the time we fell into bed, we were both physically and emotionally exhausted.

After the ceremony, a new life with Angel and Alecia started in Vacaville. We needed a fresh start to put our apprehensions to rest. We chose a new location close enough to work at a reasonable distance from the church. The ten miles guarded us against church members dropping by for advice.

There were sparks of synergy at the beginning of the marriage. One memorable night in February 1984, I returned from a church meeting around 9 p.m. That night, Angel was extremely attentive to my words. Her focus continued as we went to bed and rested. She seemed to understand the pressure of church work and comforted me with love and kisses. This was the most intimate and receptive night we had had during those first six months.

Unfortunately, that moment of intimacy was never repeated. I don't know why, but something in Angel didn't feel the need to maintain that sweet connection. She had given me a taste of her vulnerability, but these offerings were always conditional. I don't know what I did that night or what may have been an older reason for her inhibitions, but we could never get back to that synergistic love. Even talking about intimacy was hard. I felt emotionally manipulated by Angel's whims. I thought,

"Here we go again." This marriage began to seem like a repeat of the first.

Over the six months, Angel seemed restrained. Since we didn't talk about what was causing it, I could only speculate what the reasons might be. I felt like I was walking on eggshells, trying to be an understanding husband but trying not to pry. I was hesitant to cross the invisible line she had drawn and probe further into the reasons for her emotional distance. My mind swung from one side to the other like a pendulum, trying to figure out why Angel remained unapproachable. She had not shown this side of herself during the courtship. I wondered what the stumbling blocks might be. I searched the scriptures we both knew for clues. Even that deep source of wisdom never seemed to get us to the crux of our issues. Skirting around the root cause of our problems prevented a free flow of expression. An emotional dam was created, but I didn't understand how or why it was built. Talking about this dam only caused more tension. I didn't understand the dilemma in this early stage of marriage. But it felt like the honeymoon was over.

Chapter Twenty-One

That's a Double Standard

"The LORD detests double standards; he is not pleased by
dishonest scales."
Proverbs 20:23 NLT

My emotional intelligence and intuitive skills had dwindled alarmingly after the honeymoon phase. I thought an ongoing relationship increased one's capacity to exchange ideas, but the toxicity of this marriage killed every skill I had previously acquired. I didn't understand why I had to work so hard to communicate. I wanted to spend quality time engaged in lively conversation. Instead, our verbal exchanges were stuck in the Saharan desert like a jeep out of gas.

I would usually initiate: "Angel, how was your day?"

"Fine, nothing special, just the usual."

Because I had been to Angel's job, I knew the Food Bank's routine, so I dug a little deeper.

"Is Jim still having problems with the forklift?"

"Yes," Angel answered.

Her one-word responses short-circuited every desire for animated dialogue. These short, non-communicative answers were not how Angel had responded during our courtship. I felt I had been duped. It appeared she had given an Oscar performance to entice me into marriage. She needed a dad for her daughter. She wanted a husband, but it wasn't me.

I viewed myself as an agent of peace. But instead of maturing, I found myself regressing into another lonely pattern of conflict aversion. Maintaining a peaceful disposition was imperative to counsel depressed church members, prepare Bible studies, and bring a prophetic message for Sunday morning. The challenges of married life tested my personal growth and resilience severely.

Since we had vowed to cut off former relationship ties, I trusted Angel would terminate communication with Alecia's father, Mr. G. Since arriving in California from Louisiana in high school, Angel had been raised in an Assemblies of God background, Church of Anointing (COA). COA believed in Jesus, God, and the Holy Spirit and in living the Christian life. I believed Angel had a fervent walk in the Lord and that she was a woman of the Word.

During our six-month courtship, I never asked how COA had handled her out-of-wedlock pregnancy. My conflict aversion prevented me from asking her about sources of personal or social shame. Angel was human, and humans make mistakes, but I wanted some emotional insight into this crisis in her life. I wanted to know how to respond with care concerning this factor in our life together. I lacked the spiritual maturity to navigate these muddy waters or to see how treacherous they might become. I feared if I opened this can of worms, I would not come out unscathed.

Questions about Angel's friends never entered my mind. I was either totally trusting or just naïve. I never suspected my spirit-filled Christian wife would have inappropriate relationships with anybody. I held her moral character in high esteem. My naïveté would soon be tested when the CME bishop reassigned me to Tucson, Arizona, in June 1984. I was not shocked about the reassignment. In November 1983, I sensed in my spirit that God was going to move me from St. Stephen's to a new location. That supernatural revelation was the reason I felt such a need to get married. I didn't want to go to a new location as a single pastor. Research and experience have shown that the relational pressures of ministry are more difficult when the pastor is single and doesn't have a helpmate. I already knew this first-hand from sixteen months of solo ministry.

In June 1984, Angel, Alecia, and I moved to Tucson. Phillips Temple was the first church I served in an unfamiliar city. Once we were there, I totally depended on my wife for support. Questions about this new church community and supplementary job opportunities swirled in my head.

Angel got a job with the Community Center TCC. To bolster financial support, I got a job at the same location. While Angel held an 8 to 5 job, my work schedule was more flexible. I was hired as a GED instructor, work I appreciated as it opened an opportunity to help students in their educational pursuits.

Because of my flexible hours, one of my tasks involved going to the front of the office to retrieve messages. Angel, it turned out, often received messages from Mr. G. I didn't catch all the messages, but Mr. G was calling Angel at least five times a week. At the end of the second week of this, I confronted Angel.

"It appears Mr. G. is calling you at least once a day."

Angel said, "Mr. G. is just a friend."

I said, "He's not just a friend. He's Alecia's biological father. That's an inappropriate friendship."

Angel shrugged it off. "It's nothing to worry about."

Angel got testy about my conversation with female office workers but deflected my concerns about her ongoing communication with Mr. G. I said, "That's a double standard." I was furious with Angel at work, which spilled over to tension at home. In a coy way, Angel would make up for our disagreements about Mr. G's friendship, but inside, I knew something wasn't right. In retrospect, I reflected on the nights Angel had been emotionally restrained at our apartment in Vacaville. Was this absence of warmth going to continue in Tucson?

I wondered how long Angel would play this game of denial at work and conciliatory affection at home. Angel got pregnant in October 1984 with my first biological child, Naivasha. During this saga, I became increasingly physically tired from working two jobs and emotionally tired from dealing with the pressures of marriage.

As a result of the ongoing communication with Mr. G, Angel decided to meet him during the Christmas holidays in Arizona. This rendezvous was a complete betrayal of our marriage vows. I said to myself, "What did I get myself into? This marriage is awful, and the sadness is making ministry impossible." Preaching, teaching, and counseling about love was difficult when there was turmoil in my own home. Angel's Christmas meeting with Mr. G. forced me to return deeply depressed to the Bay Area for the holidays.

This holiday separation experience was déjà vu. In my first marriage, Jasmine and I had spent our first Christmas apart. I understood then because Jasmine wanted to be with her family. Now, in my second marriage, I didn't understand why Angel would want to spend time with a man who wasn't her husband. Why was this dilemma happening again? I gave this question serious reflection in late December.

As I flew back to Oakland, I didn't know how I would make it emotionally through the holidays. Fortunately, Yvette, my first love, was in town from Arkansas. She was a doctoral candidate at San Francisco Theological Seminary. Ironically, both of us were experiencing marital challenges.

I decided to go to Yvette's home to talk. We sat safely ten feet apart. As we commiserated, we sulked over our own problems and asked, "Why didn't we communicate about the marital difficulties we were having?"

I said, "Yvette, I respected your marriage and didn't want to ruffle any feathers."

Yvette said the same. "I knew you were married, trying to start a new marriage and ministry."

If I had known in 1983 that Yvette was having problems, I would have waited. If Yvette had known I was single, this meeting would have been a blessing instead of a discussion of marital woes. Life and timing teach harsh lessons.

After the holidays, Angel and I didn't talk about the people we had visited. She didn't talk about Mr. G., and I dared not speak of Yvette. I wanted to, but I thought Angel would throw that relationship in my face. It's sad when you can't be authentic with the person you're supposed to share your heart with.

As the new year started, the marital tensions of the past were complicated by the expectation of our new child in 1985. I read everything I could about fatherhood and went to Lamaze classes at Tucson Medical Center (TMC). Carrying a child in the heat of Tucson was challenging, but I was blessed to monitor Angel's activity since we both worked together. As the due date approached in early July, I monitored her every step. I wanted to be there when her water broke.

On July 3rd, Angel's water burst, and my whole world stopped. We rushed to TMC, called Angel's doctor, and started the long wait through dilation and labor. I knew Angel wanted to deliver this child naturally, but if the pain got too fierce, an epidural was an option. I prayed that the Lamaze class instruction would be helpful. I had heard stories of women in labor going through so much pain they would tell their husbands to leave the room. I was ready for this rejection, but thankfully, it never came. I was humbled to sit in the room and help with the breathing process. Angel and I bonded at a deeper level because of being together that day. After four hours, a baby girl, Naivasha Colette, came forth. I thought about the years I had waited and the prayers I had sent forth to experience the joy of this day. I thought about the sacrifices we both had made for this miracle. What an exciting day!

I held Naivasha, weighed her, and went down to the room where they made her first footprints. I thanked Angel with flowers and balloons and told her how much I loved her. I knew that, despite all our troubles, this was a signature moment no one could take away from us.

Chapter Twenty-Two

Eight Hundred at Work and Four at Home

"Do not neglect the gift that is in you, which was given to you by prophecy."
1 Timothy 4:14a

The reassignment to Tucson was a prophecy fulfilled. God spoke to me in 1983 that a geographical move was coming. My spirit responded, "Get married to prepare for this manifestation." I did not want to move to a new church and reenter the rigors of dating in a new city. Pastoring my first church in Fairfield as a single man was challenging. I needed a prayer warrior, Bible-believing, intercessory helpmate. I believed Angel was that person and that our marriage in 1984 was the will of God.

Naivasha's birth helped heal the four-year wound left by Dad's passing. Her birth on July 3rd, 1985, echoed Dad's birthdate of July 2nd. Through her smiles, I imagined Dad being resurrected in human form. I dedicated her life with renewed dedication to her mother. I ensured milk bottles were ready for midnight feeding and sound monitors were appropriately placed if her asthma flared up.

Even as I pastored Phillips Chapel in Tucson, other career options filled my mind. In the Methodist church, pastors are required to be available for reassignment at any point. This was my second church in two years, and I questioned my bishop's utilization of my skills. Most pastors I knew had been at their churches for years without being moved. Why was I the itinerant lone wolf? My father's losing his church abruptly on his last assignment at the whim of his bishop left me apprehensive that trauma was on the way. The fear of a similar incident motivated me to keep an eye out for vocational possibilities.

One of my seminary friends, Roland Ruffin, went directly from seminary into prison ministry. Whenever I spoke with him, he encouraged me to change directions.

"Roland, I wish I had some stability in ministry!"

"Man, Rob, you need to try the Department of Corrections. We've got great benefits, with two days a week off, paid travel, and sick leave."

"Let me know if there's an opening! Moving around every two years is hard for family adjustment."

An opportunity came in August 1986 that allowed me to interview at Folsom State Prison in California. Roland was on the panel and felt I interviewed well. When I returned to Tucson, a letter arrived indicating I had scored in the ninety-second percentile. That risk was one of the best strategic moves in my life.

When the Annual Conference (AC) occurred on August 31st, I was glad the interview scores were part of my resume. The AC transferred me back to California to pastor my third church in four years, Stewart Memorial, Pittsburg. This was a loving church, but the parsonage was a problem. The palm tree in the front yard affected the plumbing. We had to wait on the Trustees to resolve this and every other structural issue. This fifty-year-old home was in the roughest socio-economic section of the city. The downtrodden often knocked on our door at 10 p.m. to get food vouchers. These folks knew the property well. One night, someone even removed the bars and stole our television and jewelry.

Considering these church and parsonage concerns, I interviewed for a prison job without guilt. I felt this opportunity was an answer to prayer. Though the Northern California Women's Facility (NCWF) was an hour's drive away, I believed God used this to bring harmony to our family. After the interview, NCWF offered me the Protestant Chaplain position on an intermittent basis. I started in September 1987, three months before the prison opened. I told Angel this was our chance to get out of the cycle of being reassigned, and she agreed to relocate. My heart wanted to stay at Stewart Memorial, but getting out of the vicious cycle of itinerant ministry was exhilarating. We couldn't wait for the fiscal year's end, so in the spring of 1988, we moved six miles east to Antioch. Though the space was smaller, the apartment was fresh and safe. When the Conference rolled around in July, I had already given notice to the Presiding Elder about full-time work at NCWF.

As we moved to Antioch, Angel was four months pregnant with our youngest child, Kayla. As we settled into our new place, we prepared for a newborn again. We knew that eventually moving to Stockton was inevitable. The drive was a hardship, and the work shift was lengthy, from 12 noon to 8:30 p.m., sometimes longer. I often got sleepy driving home to Antioch from Stockton.

I didn't tell Angel about the sleepy driving mishaps but resolved those issues silently by getting an inexpensive flat in Stockton. I didn't discuss this with Angel because I knew she would get upset. I wanted to maintain peace, marital harmony, and minimal stress for Angel in her months of pregnancy. Thankfully, Kayla was born in a familiar hospital, Vallejo Kaiser. I was glad to be in the birthing room again to help Angel with her breathing.

As I kept the home front safe, there was prison activity inside the walls. After reading *Games Criminals Play* during Employee Orientation, my intuition for institutional life evolved. Every time I stepped in the yard, at least three of the inmates asked me for something illegal before I got to my office. I learned to say "No" instinctively to eliminate any appearance or thought of impropriety. Other personnel did not have the discipline to thwart this onslaught of inmate requests.

During the first season of Lent at NCWF in 1988, the Protestant department planned a dramatic presentation around the Resurrection theme. The play was filled with songs, disciples, soldiers, a crucifixion, and a resurrection. On Easter morning, 300 inmates flowed into the gymnasium at 9:45 a.m. for the 10 o'clock worship service. Suddenly, there was a commotion in the nearby outside restroom. Correctional officers sprinted to the scene of the incident and told us to stop everything. A command was voiced, "Inmates face down on the ground!" I found out later that two inmates were involved in cutting another woman. One inmate was on the lookout, while the other cut the face of the victim. It was apparently a love triangle. The investigation revealed that "the cutting device came from a staff member." The incident put my intuition on red alert.

Nevertheless, I stayed. Needing a larger home, we moved to a condo in Stockton in 1989. NCWF was only twenty minutes away, and the school for the kids was so close they could walk. I often dropped them off in the morning.

Stockton had a history of crime, and we were not immune, so we continually prayed. A pivotal incident occurred on a Friday afternoon in August. While I was seated in the living room watching television, I heard a loud noise outside where my car was parked. In my mind, I realized I had to decide: either go outside and investigate at the risk of bodily harm or stay inside and see what happens. I chose the latter. When I ventured outside, my red Camaro was gone. I didn't panic. I felt blessed to have followed my intuition. We reported the theft to the police, and three hours later, they called to tell us the whole story. Two persons had stolen the car, run a couple of red lights, parked the car, and left. The police were still in pursuit of the car thieves.

The next day, the police dropped my car off with a police report. The insurance company reported damages of six hundred dollars, a small price to pay for personal safety. Lessons learned: let the Holy Spirit guide and your family will be protected.

And they were, though not without some costly life challenges. Several months later, I was involved in a life-changing car accident that left me with recurring back pain and other issues. During my hospitalization, my wife visited only once. The experience exposed the degree to which our relationship had degenerated.

Though I was working hard, I felt led to go back for postgraduate studies. I wanted to improve my pastoral care skills and prepare for what God had in store. I worked on my degree for five years, finally matriculating at the Golden Gate Baptist Theological Seminary, where my father had received his Master's in Religious Education. I thought the Doctor of Ministry program was perfect because I didn't have to attend every day, and the State of California paid for one month of educational leave. Scheduling was difficult, but I believed the effort paid off.

In the daily grind of having eight hundred women at work and four at home, Angel suggested I needed to be around men. I agreed and knew being around only one gender was not healthy. That mutual decision changed our lives. I acted quickly on her suggestion. In November 1992, I went to the Alameda Naval Base and spoke with a recruiter about chaplaincy in the Navy. After a background check and interview, I received a Commission on March 22nd, 1993, at my home.

This turning point decision meant more than being a soldier. I understood what it meant to be a "good soldier of Jesus Christ" putting on the whole armor of God. But I also felt this position gave me insight into battles that go on daily between the flesh and the spirit.

Chapter Twenty-Three

Things I Don't Write About

"Hear, my son, and be wise; and guide your heart in the way."
Proverbs 23:19

There were things I wanted at home that I only seemed to get at work.

At home, I wanted to be heard, seen, and accepted. Within the confines of my abode, I wanted my wife to sit and listen to every word that flowed from my velvet lips. I wanted her to be present, close enough to graze the whiskers on my face and blow away the curl in my hair. So close I could light up her heart by simply opening my eyes and pursing my lips. I wanted her to sit with bated breath and adore me for all my splendor and imperfections. I wanted to define and redefine our love, one day and one word at a time. I wanted all the love that was possible from one woman to one man. I wanted to be her first choice, her one-of-a-kind. I wanted her to lay aside every thought of another man, every suitor who had ever tried to lure her, and accept my daily gestures of romance, enticement, and embrace. As the country shepherd from the Bayou, I wanted to share my love with this country girl from Louisiana. I wanted the holy fire that burned in my heart to be placed on the sacred hearth of righteous love. Because I didn't get that at home, the unsatisfied part of me longed to receive some semblance of it at work. This was a prayer. Even in my spiritual mindset, I thought I deserved some emotional validation.

Usually, I get from work what I didn't get at home. Before going to work, I put on the whole armor of God so that I was ready to respond to any situation. I prepared my day with prayer, scripture reading, and Bible study. I walked into the lion's den every day, but my eyes were turned toward Yeshua. At work, eight hundred women were waiting to engage me. Waiting to ask me, "How was your day?" They stood in anticipation, wanting a conversation with a good and honest man, yearning to look into my eyes, carry my bags, and get a scent of my cologne. I felt like a king with ladies in waiting. Daily they remained to ask me how they could make me happy and lighten my load. They waited, one, two, and sometimes three in a posse. They stuck around to butter me up so I could listen to their stories one at a time.

They waited to experience sunshine through my eyes, a flower through my words, or a butterfly through the movement of my hands. They expected me to part the clouds and jumpstart the roller coaster of their heart. Each of them wanted a fresh, restorative moment with a man. I believed their hearts wanted to have honest communication without lust, money, or sexual favors.

Yes, they lingered in full array, white, black, brown, and yellow in every hair color, brunette, blond, and redhead, from Mexico, Cuba, and Ukraine. They approached me just to be recognized. They entered my space, waiting for friendship I could not give, expecting to be healed from the past, hoping for redemption. They came walking, whispering, wooing to be set free from their guilt. Because these women could not get over the physical barbed wire, maybe a conversation with the chaplain would give them hope enough to dream again. They came desiring anything that would remove the pain, stop the bleeding, and help them reclaim their humanness.

My sanctified mind yearned to be the liberator. I wanted to be their touchstone, their knight in shining armor, to remove the albatross from their necks. I wanted to be what they had been looking for all their life. I yearned to model Boaz as they prepared themselves for wholesome relationships. I desired to be the blessing that would allow them finally to exhale. I realized this task was too much for one man. I was not naïve.

After the third month of their neediness, I realized I could not be their savior or redeemer. I realized that these women needed God-fearing women to lead them to a place of redemption. This was the greatest epiphany of this ministry at NCWF, and it was transformative for all of us. When I read that 97% of women incarcerated had been molested, I knew my ministry strategy had to change. The true deliverance of the incarcerated women would be facilitated by godly women volunteers led by the Holy Spirit. This truth was the clear message that kept the ministry moving forward. We trained four hundred women each year who entered the facility with specific ministry goals. I felt blessed that God gave me the wisdom to provide administrative orientation for these anointed volunteers. My role was to facilitate and guide them in the daily challenges of discipleship. Their diligence and dedication helped to fulfill God's direction given to me, that the prison needed to be closed.

Chapter Twenty-Four

Not Mutual, But I Will Acquiesce

"And a husband is not to divorce his wife."
1 Cor. 7:11b

One of the benefits of two jobs was building a financial base. Potential home ownership was a hurdle we still needed to clear. Going through this process seemed like generational déjà vu. My parents had gone through a similar dilemma. After living in the Minden and Shreveport parsonages, Mom lost her patience with a third parsonage in Oakland. She wanted home ownership and equity. She even used my classmate's scrimmages to pursue her dream. She used the bullying I encountered at school to lobby for a move to the hills. Her desire was so strong it created conflict among ecclesiastical leadership. My mother's relentless pursuit of her dream eventually got my father in trouble with the Presiding Bishop. Pursuing independent home ownership broke a precedent for ministers, which was mandatory residence in the parsonages where they pastored. Bishop Amos used this ecclesiastical statue to take my father's church away from him.

Angel and I did not have any disagreement on this issue. We both knew the advantages of home ownership, and I believed we were together for the long haul. I had no desire to leave Angel, although I didn't know then, in 1993, about her hidden agenda. Homeownership may have been a pre-mediated move toward the debacle that occurred in 1999.

My main concern about this new lifestyle was evolving adaptation. I adjusted to the complicated scheduling between NCWF, the Navy Reserves, and quality time with the family. I felt the strenuous juggling was necessary to keep career options open. It was a difficult adjustment from the regular rhythm of a single job, but I felt Angel understood my commitment to feed, clothe, and provide for our brood.

For job security, I completed my Doctor of Ministry degree in May 1994. This was a life-long dream. It took five years, but I was able to use my life-changing work experience to complete the degree. I believe the degree paid dividends as it lent credibility to my pursuit of a higher rank in the Navy. With my degree, I was entitled to wear Dad's three-striped clergy robe. My sense of accomplishment was amplified when my dissertation was housed in the Golden Gate Baptist Seminary library and the catalog of the Graduate Theological Union.

For six years, I maintained a diligent schedule. Sunday through Thursday, I worked from 12 noon to 8:30 p.m., and once a month, I went to Alameda for Navy drill. Twice a year, I performed my two-week Active-Duty Training (ADT) in my assigned unit and tried to find another set of 2-week orders elsewhere.

On Fridays and Saturdays, I was home for family time or date night. I loved reading and listening to my children express the joys of learning. I loved seeing them transform right before my eyes. Each daughter developed in her own unique way. Of course, the younger ones wanted to be like Alecia, the oldest, then fourteen, because that's what siblings do. Alecia loved to run, Naivasha, eleven, was great at gymnastics, and Kayla, eight, was great at whatever she put her mind to. I appreciated my family so much that I invited them to come to NCWF so the inmates might get a glimpse of my daily life. They came, and we had a lively discussion about that experience.

In 1995, an opportunity arose that allowed a change to a normal 8-to-5 schedule. Having more time with Angel and the kids improved family dynamics. Silently, another desire was growing in my heart. When I was first hired at NCWF, God gave me seven tasks to complete. The first six, which I have already mentioned, could be communicated to anyone. The seventh was so big, so daunting, I couldn't tell anyone. The seventh imperative was, "Close the prison!" My godly instruction was to stay at NCWF until it closed or no longer existed. So, I accepted a job as the Community Resources Manager (CRM) to ensure God's wishes would be prophetically fulfilled. I was divinely inspired to accept this mandate.

Part of my job involved moving my office from inside prison walls to the foyer. That was a relief. I had gotten tired of rebuffing verbal assaults by the inmates. I paced my emotional energies between dealing with the executive staff and the population in the yard. Because all NCWF wardens were female, I had to adjust to being near my direct supervisor. I had never been in this position. I had to keep a close watch on my behavior with each encounter; the environment was strangely sexually charged. The difficulty involved being professional enough to keep a suitable distance but loose enough to laugh comfortably when appropriate. It was especially challenging when the wardens reached out to hug me. I had to be welcoming but cautious at the same time. Maintaining that balance was taxing.

During my eight-year reign as the CRM, the wardens were receptive to my program ideas and implemented all of them. Some of the programs included "Dress for Success," which encouraged volunteers to bring in normal clothes as an alternative to the inmate's state-issued parole garments. A second program was called "Adults Molested as Children." This was a continuing eight-week program facilitated by the Women's Center in Stockton. As I mentioned, 97% of women prisoners were molested as children, and the trauma of this abuse caused nightmares and ongoing psychological and mental health issues. The objective of the programs was to reduce the recidivism rate at the prison. Third, we instituted a "DMV/Identification Program" that ensured every parolee had a valid ID or driver's license to move into an apartment or get a job. Fourth, we organized half-way houses throughout the 58 counties in California to ensure inmates had an alternative place to live instead of returning to their dysfunctional homes.

Though the inmate programs were in full swing and proving successful, my marriage had increasing challenges. For two years, from 1997 to 1999, I supported Angel's desire to pursue her Certified Nursing Assistant license. In 1999, she pursued a nursing degree at Delta Community College. I supported her financially because I knew she was following her dream. I felt my commitment to helping her fulfill her life goals would bring us closer in the long run. I also felt my change to a day shift would create more family time.

Unfortunately, one evening in September 1999, as I prepared a sermon in the study, Angel came in and announced, "I don't love you anymore." I was speechless. I knew things were bad, but I had no idea they were this bad. I didn't argue because I felt Angel's discouraging words were fully intentional. After going into prayer, I knew one of the best ways to deal with the pain in my heart was journaling, which prompted this poem.

Not Mutual…But I Will Acquiesce

My desire to divorce is not mutual,
but I will acquiesce, at your request,
It is clear I can not make you happy,
And if I can not make you happy,

You are not compelled to make me happy.
But I will acquiesce at your request.

Because my smile makes you frown,
My joy makes you depressed,
My prayers have no effect,
My preaching makes you leave the room,
So, I will acquiesce to your request,

Because I can do no right in your eyes,
No money, no floral arrangement,
No words or expression
can heal the pain of your heart and spirit.
So, I will acquiesce at your request.

Not because I want to, not because I am compelled to,
But because it is what you want,
And nothing I do changes your feelings towards me,
Because I will always forgive you,
because That's the way I do,

I will always look beyond your faults and see your needs,
And because your need is to divorce,
I will acquiesce to your request.

Words shared with Angel did not change her mind. She was adamant and dead-set on this change. I told her I would move out because it was easier for me to relocate than for her and the children. I found an apartment that was ten minutes away from the house. There was no fanfare, just a simple move. I took cooking appliances, my computer, and some clothes. I had given sixteen years to this marriage, but Angel's words set me on another path.

Had I known earlier what forces were at work in my marriage, I might have gone for marital counseling. I might have prayed more or put myself on a fast. I realized there was a "spirit of division" in the house. After living there for two years, it was confirmed the prior couple had moved out because of a horrible divorce. I regret not attacking this "spirit of division." I fell on my spiritual sword by not taking the divisive spirit seriously. I could have stood on the words of James: "Out of the same mouth comes blessing and cursing" (James 3:10). It would have been an opportune time to yield my tongue to the Holy Spirit and ensure Angel did the same. Like Adam, who allowed Eve to be unsupervised with the serpent, I took responsibility for allowing those divisive influences to linger in Angel's heart.

Chapter Twenty-Five

Moving On Despite the Pain

"And the Lord God said, 'It is not good that man should be alone; I will make him a helper comparable to him.'"
Genesis 2:18

I was blessed to get an apartment so close to my home on White Water Lane. I wanted to visit the children frequently but encountered resistance from my separated wife. I hated being away from the girls. Apartment dwelling, though, gave me private time to pray, meditate, and put my life in order.

But I was love-starved. I took full responsibility for my inability to express my desires clearly in our marriage. The tension between us had atrophied my communicative skills. When I asked for love, it was not heard. I know love involves mutual understanding, but my efforts were rarely reciprocated. Our separation eventually allowed me to reenter the dating scene. It was clear Angel had no desire to reconcile with me. When she said, "I don't love you," I interpreted those words to mean "I hate you." I, in turn, had no desire to win Angel's love again. Some may have faulted me because I didn't fight for our marriage. But I was not going to fight for more abuse. Who does that? If Angel could not recognize my commitment during the sixteen years of our marriage, she would never acknowledge my authenticity.

I took account of my loneliness and realized the only way my life was going to change was to establish relationship goals. I let a few women know that I was living a single life. I shared that information with two individuals to see what their response would be.

One was a beautiful, tall African-American Sergeant whom I worked with daily on gate clearances. She often said to me, "If you weren't married, I would give you a run for your money." I never knew what she meant, but when I told her I was single, I expected her eyes to light up. But the Sergeant never took my compliments seriously during this season of inquiry. Another interesting woman was a rehab counselor named Syn, who worked on the yard. She stopped by my office every day before going home and appreciated my escorts to her car. Her eyes sparkled every time we talked. Her desire to speak to me gave me everything I needed at the time.

As a result of Syn's constant interest, I decided to take a chance. I liked her for several reasons. At 5-feet-10-inches, she was alluring. She was a gorgeous Hawaiian Afro-American blend with high cheekbones, dimples, and short wavy hair. Syn was easy on the eyes, and I couldn't wait to place my lips on that honey-dipped dimple. My one concern was traveling 32 miles to visit her after hours. After a long day, I usually went home, got a meal, freshened up, took a nap, and headed to her place 35 minutes away. I spent a few hours in her company, getting to know her, and headed back to my apartment. In my experience, individuals who worked with women's programs often had personal challenges. As Syn spoke, she explained her backstory in depth. She even shared that she had been incarcerated and her husband had been killed. Both facts raised "red flags." I had had personal experiences with ex-cons, and none of them were positive.

I continued to spend time with her, nevertheless, and let the relationship run its course. One of the main desires she discussed was glamming up to visit a restaurant in San Francisco. I allowed her to organize the entire December evening because this was her fantasy. Though the night was chilly, our wool coats shielded us from the moist air. Syn was especially captivating that night. She needed no makeup, eyeliner, or lipstick because she was a natural beauty. She wore a burgundy sequin sparkle dress, flared at the bottom, with long sheer sleeves. I wore my black double-breasted tuxedo, with burgundy bow tie and vest. We were red carpet-ready and looked elegant. This evening revived my joy. I was happy once again to be with someone who appreciated my presence and love.

The blessing of our relationship was underscored when Syn said she had given up on men, but my kindness gave her renewed hope that she could love again, even if our relationship did not last. That statement was a high-water mark of our relationship. We never really know, at the time, why people enter our lives. I felt vindicated that I had had a restorative impact on a woman's life again. After her "renewed hope" comment, I understood why she seemed tentative. Syn was continually checking her thoughts and actions with me. Ours was the first relationship she had had since her husband was killed. Our time together combined grief, healing, acceptance, and renewal. Our relationship was a confidence builder. I knew in the eyes of God, our intimacy might not be holy, but I had spent so much time serving God that I prayed for a little grace. God showed grace by allowing this relationship to last three months into the middle of February. Syn's affection gave me faith that a woman could still be attracted to me.

Before the next relationship, I was asked to preach at my father's church, Church of All Faiths, in March. I probably prayed more in preparation for this sermon than ever before. I knew I was not living a holy life. I hoped through repentance, my inner turmoil would not be apparent in my preaching delivery.

I believed God would bless my desire to proclaim the "Good News."

I do not remember what the title or text was, but it was a theme appropriate for the annual R. Colby Thomas Scholarship program. Every year since Dad's death, my mother had organized a program to assist seminarians in pursuit of theological training. We held that service on the second Sunday of March because that was near the date around Dad's earthly departure. After the sermon, I was greeted by several persons in the church's foyer. One of them was an old family friend named Rita. We would meet informally when our families would get together. Rita had the fruits of the spirit operating in her life. Having confessed Christ at an early age, she had not only heard my father preach but always showed up when I proclaimed the Word. We had known each other for thirty-five years because her mother and my mother had been friends since 1952. We were such good friends that we had code names for each other. Though I was taller and younger, she called me "little brother," and I called her "little sister."

As I drove back to Stockton, I decided to take a detour to Antioch and parked in front of Rita's house. I prayed because she had no idea I was dropping by and prepped my emotions in case she had a visitor. I called on my cell phone and let her know I was sitting in front of her house on the opposite side of the street. She said, "Knock on the door." I could not believe the reception I received. Rita fed me, took a few photos, and, to my surprise, sat comfortably in my lap. Wow! Though we had known each other for years, this was the first time in our long acquaintance she had ever shown affection. I was giddy. This was another positive sign that women could still appreciate me.

Though it was not my intention, I did not return to my apartment that evening. Rita opened her heart and told me, "I have always liked you, but my marriage and your marriages prevented me from sharing the desires of my heart." Now, it appeared that we were both free, so we let our emotions fly in ways I could have never fathomed. During the first week after March 12th, I visited her one time in mid-week before our weekend rendez-vous. She arranged for us to visit the Embassy Suites for the weekend and attend church afterward.

Chapter Twenty-Six

Looking for a Sign

"How much better than wine is your love."
Song of Songs 4:10b

The euphoria I felt with Rita didn't allow for much reflection. We were moving at jet speed! After our rendezvous at the Embassy Suites, we traveled to Missionary Temple CME. This church was part of our DNA. When my mother was pregnant with me, she attended this household of faith and befriended Rita's mom. Furthermore, Dad received his elder's orders at this church, the September before my birth. Our time during the worship service that day was filled with deep emotions—poignant, joyful, and grateful. I enjoyed the fellowship, but the intensity of the relationship clouded my judgment. I prayed that God would forgive our cravings and see the intentions of our hearts. After the service, Rita introduced me to fellow members of the choir. She was not ashamed of letting others know she had a man. The pastor even asked if I would come back and preach. This weekend seemed too good to be true.

One conversation that raised some apprehension was Rita's mention of being a minister's wife.

She said, "I don't think I would be a good minister's wife!"

"What are some of your fears?"

"The clothes I wear and my free spirit might clash with the rules of the CME church."

I told her, "I'd never put you in a compromising situation that would limit your liberty in Christ or with fellow Christians."

I realized there were deeper issues behind her remarks, but she could not express them. I assured her she would make an excellent minister's wife because in the 35 years I had known her, she had always shown dedication: whatever she said, she did.

That Sunday evening, we went to the radio station because she had to do a broadcast. I got to meet her supervisor, who used to be Rita's boyfriend. My eyes and ears were fully engaged during our brief encounter. I realized I might find myself entangled in a web that I might not easily extricate myself from.

After the broadcast, we returned to her place and talked about how to spend the next week. I had a Navy drill near Seattle. She said, "I want to spend another weekend with you." So, we booked flights that would maximize our time together. When Friday rolled around, I took a flight from Sacramento in the afternoon and picked up a rental car to get the room prepared. I picked up flowers and met Rita at the airport. As we traveled to the hotel, her eyes twinkled as though this experience was magical. Though it had been a long day, we didn't feel exhausted. We felt fortunate to spend time together. The next morning, watching me put on my Navy khaki uniform, she said, "I like men in uniforms." The Saturday drill was difficult because I hadn't gotten quality sleep. I was glad to return to Rita's arms after a long day of training.

We didn't have anything planned for the evening, so we flowed with spontaneity. The one activity we loved was dancing. We found a dance hall that advertised a band. We got a table and drinks. When the music came on, we were the only couple on the floor. We needed room as she challenged me to show off my dance repertoire. I remember Rita saying, "And you can dance, too!" as though she had found an unexpected treasure. We swayed and whirled for two hours. It seemed like fifteen minutes. Then we drove around the brightly lit city. We wanted to go to the Space Needle but decided just to spend time at the waterfront. After returning to the hotel, we strategized how to get her to the airport the next day. We found a bus that would take her to the airport after I picked her up at the hotel after training. Even though we knew we would see each other soon, it was a difficult parting.

When I got home Sunday, I called to ensure Rita had arrived safely. She said all was well; she appreciated the weekend in Seattle. The next time we spoke was Tuesday morning. I had a break and called her on my cell phone. To my surprise, her supervisor picked up the phone and said, without further greeting, "You have to stop talking to Rita, or I am going to kill you and her." Wow! I never had a death threat, but I took this one seriously. I said, "Okay." I couldn't imagine how else to respond in this unprecedented moment.

Needing some breathing room and time to think, I took my lunch break in the trailer 500 feet from my office and almost choked on my chicken sandwich. The shock of this message took my breath away and raised my blood pressure. I almost passed out from hyperventilation. My immediate response was to halt communication to protect both of us. I had been told Rita's supervisor had mental problems. I didn't want to take the risk that he might harm her. He knew where she lived and, of course, where she worked, so she was already in the lion's den.

Anxious for her safety, I cut off communications. I trusted Rita because she had managed to kick this supervisor out of her house. Now, I believed she would find a way to resolve what I hoped was a temporary impasse. I was perplexed by the threat, but resolving this dilemma involved dangers I couldn't fully comprehend. Some might call me cowardly, but I was stung with the pain of a forced separation. I didn't want to step into a hornet's nest while she continued to work within a volatile environment. It wasn't until ten years later that I found an occasion to explain to Rita what had happened. She was sad but understood my decision because her supervisor was, in fact, mentally unstable.

It took a month to process my grief after this whirlwind affair with Rita. As I thought about finding another partner, I asked myself what lessons I'd learned in my history with women. Do not enter a relationship with someone you don't know. Too much intimacy leads to decisions you might later regret. In the two weeks I had known Rita, she suggested we get married by July before our Foote Family Reunion. I told her my divorce would not be finalized until August 20th, but her urgency never really registered. I had no way of knowing at that point why Rita was in such a hurry.

I tried another strategy for starting a relationship. This time, I was determined to take it slowly and get to know the person. Another priority was asking myself how long I had known the perspective admirer. As I scanned the field, my list was short. High on it was my peaceful friend, Susan Parker. I had a meeting scheduled in Sacramento. Since I had a ritual of touching base with Susan about once a year, I decided to contact her. I called and asked her if she could have lunch. Susan was happy to join me, and we had a delicious meal. Unwilling to end the visit at that point, we decided to have dinner. I joined her that evening at her apartment on Center Parkway.

One of the first things I noticed about her apartment was that it was on the second floor. That was a sign Susan liked an elevated view. When I got up to use the lavatory, I noticed Susan had one of my favorite scripture verses framed and sitting on a little stand: "'I know the plans I have for you,' declares the Lord, 'plans to prosper you and not harm you, plans to give you hope and a future'" (Jeremiah 29: 11). As I left the entranceway to the restroom, I saw an envelope with a handwritten list of 45 traits. I asked Susan about it. She answered, "This is the list I made after a T.D. Jakes conference in 1999."

"What does the list mean?"

"I was tired of choosing guys based on external qualities, so I made a list of internal qualities," she said. As she read off the list, I checked off on each one. It appeared I qualified.

As I smiled inside because I passed another list, the song by Sade, "The Sweetest Taboo," came on the radio. In the last line, the singer says, "Every day is Christmas, and every night is New Year's Eve." I had mentioned that I didn't want to date. I wanted to get married. Listening to those lyrics, we agreed that if that was the decision we reached, we would get married on New Year's Eve. We kept that discussion to ourselves for the time being.

In the following months, I tried to spend as much time as I could with Susan. I made the drive from Stockton to Sacramento at least once during the week and spent weekends at her place unless I had a Navy drill. This was our pattern until Susan met my clan at the Family Reunion in July 2000.

When I visited Susan, one concern became a constant talking point. Often, I would spend the night, but we slept in separate bedrooms. She wanted me to respond to her sleepwear, but I put those comments and emotions on hold. I was trying to develop an appropriate relationship in the eyes of God. Both of us had been in situations where love shared would drift into intimacy. We wanted to prevent that pattern from repeating this time. Susan always looked beautiful, and I always responded, though she sometimes got upset because I didn't respond more enthusiastically. I had to remind her that we were surrendering to a higher calling. I loved everything she wore. Old patterns die hard, and I had to be sensitive when this issue arose. I reassured Susan that I was all about healthy self-esteem, but I couldn't respond as eagerly as I wanted to until we were married.

Chapter Twenty-Seven

Peace That Surpasses All Understanding

"He who finds a wife finds a good thing, and obtains favor
from the LORD."
Proverbs 18:22

The next hurdle for Susan was meeting the Foote-Steuben clan. We were the host family for the July 2000 bi-annual family reunion. Everything was organized: the hotel, the program, the food, the shuttle pick-ups. Since the divorce from Angel was pending, all of my extended family folks were excited to meet Susan. Susan felt the pressure, and I tried to be supportive as she asked questions ahead of time. I encouraged her to pitch in with preparations to alleviate her anticipatory jitters. July 2000 became a happy occasion.

However, not long after August 20th, a sad experience occurred. This was the signing day for the divorce papers. We had tried to work out our differences through pastoral counseling, but the pain was too deep. After the "I don't love you" declaration of September 1999, my heart needed time to heal. When Angel and I met for dinner in May 2000, she was hoping we would reconcile. She had never discussed reconciliation during the seven months of separation. During the divorce signing, Angel kept saying, "So we are doing this!" And I kept pointing out, "This is what you wanted." Though she was the plaintiff,

Angel could not see that she had started the divorce process, and I had grudgingly responded to her request.

Angel knew that according to biblical law, I would never divorce her. But she was divorcing me. She often said she "wanted to be happy." I responded, "If divorcing me is what you need for happiness, go ahead and file." I was not going to fight to keep living with her cantankerous behavior. Neither would I fight to regain her love because I believed that would be a losing battle. If Angel could not see that my emotional and spiritual intentions were genuine, then she would never understand. I hated that the divorce was occurring, but the change forced me to pursue avenues of self-care and personal growth. I loved being a father; one of the great costs of the divorce was the damage and trauma it brought into my relationships with my daughters. I have spent a lifetime trying to repair a trauma that did not have to happen.

After the divorce, though, my soul was free. I felt liberated from prison. In Angel's company, I could not be my authentic self. When I tried to function authentically, my efforts were squashed. I felt I had done everything within my God-given power to love and provide for my family. My inability to have a real, two-way conversation with her about my discontentment and discouragements had cost me my marriage. That failure to confront situations head-on made Angel think I was a pushover. She often said she had lost respect for me. Hearing those words was the ultimate depressant. Her contempt for me made her feel she could treat me any way she wanted. But I was not a dishrag and didn't deserve this irreverence. I yearned for someone who would be kinder and gentler in talking over difficulties. I believed I had found that person in Susan.

I met Susan in 1992 at NCWF. She worked as the Procurement Officer when I served as the Protestant Chaplain. When I needed extra Bibles, I could not acquire them through donations. She approved the money from our Chaplain budget. I noticed then her calm demeanor as she floated through her office. As I waited in her cubicle for her to complete the necessary forms, Susan would share her love for travel and adventure. These easy conversations resonated with my spirit. Though she was at NCWF for only two years, the peace of these brief encounters stayed with me. Between 1994 and 2000, I met up with her at her new workplace for lunch to catch up. I never imagined we would be together. I just knew Susan complimented me.

After dating for six months, Susan and I made plans to go to Burney Falls for a camping trip. This was our second outing. She had said how much she loved the outdoors. I was pleasantly surprised she was so adventurous. That was one of the disappointments in living with Angel. She never wanted to go anywhere with me, and many opportunities and memories were missed as a result. Though Susan thought this was just another camping trip, I used it as an opportunity to propose. We arrived on Friday. On Saturday, we took a walk down the trail to the river. On the rocks near the falls, I got down on one knee. Susan pulled me up, thinking I was stumbling, but I knelt back down. I reached into my pocket and pulled out a ring I had carefully tucked there. I asked her, "Susan, will you marry me?" Thankfully, she said, "Yes," as she reached out a second time to steady me. We often laughed about this moment because she really thought I was falling. But That's how memories should be. We should be able to take the most memorable event and turn it into a smile. This type of adventure was what I hoped would be the signature feeling of our relationship.

One of my final family tests came a month later—meeting Susan's mother, Bessie Wade, and her sister, Judie, in Rocky Mount, Virginia. It was a joyous occasion to meet individuals who had spent their life in church. I was born into the church and spent at least two out of seven days in the church throughout my life. Wherever individuals are praying and praising

God, we are brothers and sisters in Christ. I believed Mother Wade liked me because of the little things she would do when I was there. She felt comfortable sitting next to me, praying and singing *Songs of Zion*. Being with Susan's family seemed like a week at home. Out of all the encounters I had had with in-laws, this was the best. The family seemed genuine in their faith, walk, and practical response to the Gospel. Susan's family of origin and church family recognized the joy of the Lord in my life. I felt our relationship was strengthened by the visit to Rocky Mount.

As we talked about a day to get married, we reflected on the first evening we had spent together. Here again, one of the lines in Sade's "The Sweetest Taboo" became significant: "Every day is Christmas, and every night is New Year's Eve." So, we set December 31st as our marriage date. We thought about the best way to celebrate and organize the day. This was going to be the third marriage for both of us, so we decided that we should keep the event small and intimate. We felt we should spend more resources on the honeymoon than the wedding. We looked for a chaplain and a place. Since I supervised several chaplains at NCWF, Chaplain Zachary was an easy selection who gladly accepted my invitation. During Navy drills, I spent several drill weekends at Coast Guard Petaluma. The chapel was rarely used but beautifully decorated. I scheduled the chapel for 3 p.m. On the actual date, we asked my mom and one of Susan's friends, Gene, to be the witnesses. It was a beautiful, simple wedding followed by a celebration dinner at a local restaurant. We stayed at the Coast Guard Quarters to consummate our lovely marriage.

From my perspective, the honeymoon we planned was the honeymoon I had always wanted. I love to celebrate, and six years of Navy training in Hawaii made me feel Oahu and the islands were my second home. We stayed in the Hale Koa Hotel and traveled to all my favorite locations. Every morning and every sunset was filled with precious and everlasting memories. It was a joy to sit and look at the beaches, smell the plumeria, and watch doves alight on the balcony rails with Susan. I had spent time on beaches and in the mountains, hoping one day I could spend time in those beautiful places with my bride. The best way I could commemorate my time in Hawaii was a poem that still makes me think of the sunsets we shared.

Love Sonnet Number Seven

I do not love you like a cloudy sunset that fades
into a forgettable horizon,
I love you like the tranquil blue inside the twilight,
when the pink glow passes through space,
scattering its hue in the atmosphere.

I love you like dew-kissed roses,
Nurtured and trusted, perfumed
With sweet fragrance, in perpetual bloom.
I love you without knowing the chilly dawn or
shadowy dust of tomorrow.
Time stops.
When your heart winks, my smile widens,
Igniting the wave of love
that began with volcanic urges.

Grasp my hand with all your fingers,
and touch the layers of petals inside our rosette,
The bright, waning sun approaches a memorable vista,
Waiting for our love to color the sky!

Chapter Twenty-Eight

The Prophecy Is Fulfilled

"Blessed be the Lord, for He has shown me His marvelous kindness in a strong city!"
Psalm 31:21

We started our married life in Sacramento. This was a shift after twenty years in Stockton. It has taken a long time to understand the swag of this city. I'm still trying to find the pilot light that keeps this town robust. As I struggled to meet the challenge of yet another adjustment, I couldn't wait to remove the things I had from storage. Though I loved being with Susan, I was discouraged that I couldn't hang all my clothes up. The lack of storage space in our 950-square-foot apartment motivated us to move. After looking for two months, we eventually found a home in Galt. We learned a lot about our similarities and differences in the process of house hunting. We grew through dialogue as we worked out compromises about what we each wanted in a home. I wanted a big garage and yard. She wanted spacious bedrooms.

We decided on a home in Galt with a small porch and a huge backyard. Susan appreciated the open kitchen and family room, which encouraged entertaining. The problem we eventually discovered about this home was not apparent during a walk-through: it could only be detected by daily use. Since birth, I have had slightly impaired hearing. In elementary school, swollen adenoids blocked my inner ear structure. Playing music in school and marching bands exposed me to loud decibels week after week. The real damage occurred in the military when I was assigned to howitzer units for four years. The repeated blasts of the artillery led to 24/7 tinnitus and partial loss of hearing. Unfortunately, we found out too late we were located next to a commuter route that was a lot busier than we'd imagined. The noise level, combined with the closure of NCWF prison, encouraged us to move again eighteen months later to Fairfield, CA.

Eight months into our marriage, the second pastor of the Church of All Faiths (COAF), which Dad co-founded, died. Several thoughts ran through my head concerning this transition in the life of that church. After arriving at the hotel in Oakland for my monthly drill, I woke at 3 a.m. and penned the letter to COAF, which I mentioned earlier. It included condolences, praise for the years of leadership the pastor had provided after Dad's death, and my intention to be of service to the church, though emphatically not as their pastor. I concluded with a prayer for their peace in transition. By now, I knew a lot about transitions.

As I mentioned, I never sent it. It stated the true intention of my heart, but my mother was still living, and she persuaded me to apply for the pastor position. Three months later, I interviewed for it and was selected as one of two final candidates. I had mixed feelings: this was the church that killed Dad. Throughout my subsequent ministry at COAF, I said to the congregation, "I love you, but you're not going to kill me."

In January 2002, I started pastoring at COAF against my better judgment. Pastoring is not about self. It's about being God-centered. This developed into the most hectic job schedule of my life. I had three jobs: working at the prison, Navy Reserves drills once a month, and now the church. Each job required hours of close attention to tasks and people. I was wrestling with what felt like a three-headed monster.

On February 28th, 2003, in my second year of pastoring, NCWF closed. This was a fulfillment of the directive God had given me sixteen years previously. In 1987, God had given me very clear mandates pertaining to my work at the prison, the final of which was "Close the prison."

The backstory to my work reveals why prison ministry was a divine match for me. In my freshman year of college, I took the Minnesota Multiphasic Psychological test to determine my career affinities. The results indicated I should be a Female Staff Sergeant—a confusing result! I chalked that result up to testing irregularities. Four years later, I took the same test, and the results indicated the same career path: Female Staff Sergeant. For sixteen years, from 1971 to 1987, I wondered what these statistical results meant. What I surmised was that I had the heart to listen to women's concerns and the wisdom to guide them toward the lifestyle choices they needed.

Ministry at the women's facility was a calling, not a job. An extra ounce of my fiber was focused on fulfilling God's seven-fold mission plan. I worked so diligently that it caused problems in my second marriage. At times, I worked more than forty-hour weeks. I had co-dependency issues that showed up in my workaholic behavior. We had three services on Sunday, Bible Studies every Wednesday, and Women's Aglow deliverance services monthly.

I took a special interest in every inmate. At least twice a week, a bus came to NCWF from the County Jail with new inmates. I retrieved the institutional list from the yard sergeant, got a barrel of literature, and introduced myself to the women with evangelistic zeal through a four-by-two-foot metal gate. By using the inmate list, I tried to increase their self-esteem by learning their names, not their five-digit CDC number. This was my script for the new arrivals. As I listened to each inmate's reason for being incarcerated, I would say, "This is the last time you will be here!" I tried to plant a seed of hope that would help them change their paradigm. I realized inmates often recidivated because they had no support or returned to a dysfunctional home situation. My goal was to get women home if that was a place where healing could happen, and not remain institutionalized.

We encouraged women who got off parole to come back and tell their stories about how to have a successful parole. I believe the eventual reduction of total women at the prison was a result of prayer, discipleship, and continued concern by those who ministered there.

It was my excitement to serve at NCWF that led me to decide to pursue a postgraduate degree at the Golden Gate Baptist Theological Seminary. My father had received his Master's in Religious Education at this seminary. I started there in 1989. In the third year, I chose my dissertation topic: "Self-Esteem Improvement for Incarcerated Women at the NCWF."

From my daily observations and research, I surmised one of the issues women in prison faced was low self-esteem. My goal was to advocate a theocentric approach as opposed to the humanistic approach that was generally adopted at the facility. I used quantitative and qualitative tools and a target and control group for this dissertation. Research revealed that incarcerated women's self-esteem is improved with consistent counseling, monitoring, and covenant goals.

The women's own comments about what they received were gratifying. K.C. said, "I've gone to shrinks and psychologists and have been in every kind of program…since seventeen years old. I think I accomplished more in my life in these last six months than I did in 37 years." M.F. expressed, "I don't get depressed anymore because I know it's not healthy. I liked this class because it was biblical. At first, I didn't want anybody to take this class because of jealousy…but I learned not to be jealous because I want to share with others what I have learned." These words spoke volumes about the impact listening can have in the hard process of personal recovery and growth.

Chapter Twenty-Nine

Hanging on with Hope

"And not only that, but we also glory in tribulations, knowing that tribulation produces perseverance; and perseverance, character; and character, hope."
Romans 5: 3-4

The group and individual counseling component of my research precipitated new insights. M.F. said, "The preaching, discussion groups, and counseling affected my growth." She continued, "Just from listening to the sermons in service…the Word was able to break down the walls that were hindering and keeping me from growing in my walk with the Lord." The inmates' feedback buoyed my sense of purpose at the women's prison and led me to my own fruitful self-examination. Theory plus pastoral care shifted the institutional paradigm and moved many of the women from despair to hope. The success of this work motivated poetic creativity.

God gave me a poem about Christ esteem called "The ABCs of Godly Identity."

When people ask me how I'm doing, I respond with a Godly truth,
not a worldly lie, by telling the inquirer, I'm…

Too Anointed to be Disappointed...
Too Blessed to be Stressed...
Too Consecrated to be Agitated...
Too Dedicated to be Fabricated...
Too Edified to be Crucified...
Too Forgiven to be Backslidden...
Too Glad to be Mad...
Too Healed to be Concealed...
Too Inspired to be Tired...
Too Justified to be Nullified...
Too Kept to be Inept...
Too Lifted to be Downshifted...
Too Manifested to be Detested...
Too Northward to be Downward...
Too Ordained to be Profaned...
Too Proficient to be Deficient...
Too Quickened to be Sickened...
Too Redeemed to be Declaimed...
Too Sanctified to be Mortified...
Too Transformed to be Conformed to this world...
Too United to be Divided...
Too Victorious to be Notorious...
Too Wonderfully-made to be Dismayed...
Too Exhilarated to be Humiliated...
Too Yielded to be Dismissed...
Too Zealous to be Jealous...

The pressure of performing three jobs, though, took a toll on my body. I believed the stress manifested in the form of spiritual attacks. The most anointed activity I was assigned was saving souls. During sixteen years at NCWF, I believed God had "taken back what the enemy had stolen." Over fifty percent of the original 800 incarcerated women from 1987 had been paroled. Most were in supportive communities away from an incarcerated life. Because God allowed me to trespass in Satan's territory, I was constantly under attack.

At my new prison, California Men's Facility in Vacaville, I was under extreme scrutiny. The administration felt pressured to accept me because my previous prison had closed. At this new institution, there was a spirit of pride, even in the Warden's meetings. All the key staff were arrogantly rank-conscious. Every day, there were power plays. Political decisions in Sacramento caused the department to eliminate my job classification throughout the state. After the declassification, I was shuffled among three departments. The confidence I had built up over sixteen years eroded.

One of the spiritual attacks came when I was assigned to the accounting department. My job for the day was counting pennies. This was a humbling task, but life has a way of building character. In my mind, I continued to say, "Trust in the Lord with all thine heart, and lean not unto thine own understanding, in all thy ways acknowledge him, and he shall direct thy paths" (Proverbs 3: 5-6). Sitting on a stool in front of the safe, I swiveled to the left, and my right foot went numb. I had never felt neuropathy before. It did not leave. When I saw a doctor about it one month later, he confirmed I had Type 2 diabetes. The diagnosis was worsened by the doctor's prophecy that my health would get increasingly worse. Because of my faith in prayer, I rejected the physician's gloomy prognostication. I mused, "This doctor's prophecy is from the pit of hell." In response, I began to search for a holistic doctor who would help me work toward an alternative way of living.

The next physical attack occurred one Sunday in 2005 when I preached so hard I felt something burst above my eyebrows. When I looked after the service, I noticed a ruptured blood vessel that had spread six inches. I knew I was under pressure, but nothing exemplified stress like a visible mark across my forehead. The mark stayed for six months and marred every photo

I took. Part of the reason I preached so hard was that the Church of All Faiths congregation was affected by a "spirit of error." This cloud involved resistance to Biblical truth and to the direction given in sermons.

After my Type 2 diagnosis in April 2004, it was time to get a job that matched the salary I had had as a Community Resources Manager. I searched and interviewed with the Chief Psychiatrist, Dr. Phil, for a job in Oakland as a Mental Health Program Supervisor. I believed the more I knew about mental health, the more I would understand the trauma experienced by church members and military personnel. If I got the job, it would minimize driving to church on Wednesdays and make it easier to catch the plane on Thursdays once a month to my Commanding Officer position in Phoenix, Arizona. The interview went well and I looked forward to working with the Parole Division. During the interview, I noticed a picture of a man on the interviewer's desk. I had no idea who the man was, but because of the position of the picture, I knew the person was significant.

I had no problem with other people's sexual preferences. I identified as a heterosexual male and didn't feel I had to announce that publicly or privately in a group setting. As long as one's sexual preference did not hinder their ability to perform their tasks or prevent me from performing mine, everything was copacetic. After I started as the Mental Health Supervisor, I discerned that a "perversion spirit" was overshadowing our supervisors' meetings. The supervisors' meeting included Dr. Phil, a psychologist, a Licensed Social Worker, and me. The other two supervisors were very aware of our supervisor's lifestyle and his African-American male partner, whom he eventually married. They spoke of Dr. Phil's escapades with complicity. I never understood the discrete nature of the jokes shared in the meeting until I realized the Chief's living situation. His personal life was not an issue until my supervisor gave me a book,

On the Down Low: A Journey into the Lives of Straight Black Men Who Sleep with Men. The other supervisors laughed at the gesture as though it was no big deal. Although I kept it in my office on the bottom shelf, I felt the action was sexual harassment. To add to the harassment, I felt religious harassment. One of the supervisors would often turn my mention of the word God into Dog. Eventually, Dr. Phil broke up with his partner, and I seemed to get the fallout from that failed relationship. At times, he would get angry with me for no reason, though the fact that he was Black, as I am, might account for his transferring his hostility to me. He would ask me to increase the productivity of the eleven people I supervised, knowing that request was a losing battle.

During this difficult season of multiple jobs, I had several counseling sessions with my older sister, Ronita. She provided excellent life coaching. She saw the stress that I was going through at close range.

Ronita asked the hard questions. "Robert, you can't keep going at this pace."

"Yes, I know, something has to give. This pace is killing me."

She reminded me, "I know you don't want to end up like Dad, with a shortened life span."

"Yea, I have got to quit one of these jobs, somehow." I shared some of these thoughts with Susan to get her input. Because I already had twenty years of State service and the stress of spiritual attack at Paroles, it was time to lighten my mental and emotional workload. My wife agreed, which helped me cement the decision in my heart. Fortunately, we were having one of our regional workshops, and we added my retirement to the agenda. The annual meeting turned a negative work situation into a positive one by having all the Parole clinicians there. The enthusiastic clinicians who appreciated my work gave the retirement ceremony a celebrative moment of blessing. I believed

God got the glory as I completed my California Department of Corrections & Rehabilitation employment with gratitude. I retired in July 2006 and never looked back. I ministered for sixteen years until NCWF closed, then two years at CMF and two brief years in Paroles. I felt my career with the California Department of Corrections and Rehabilitation was complete.

Energetically, I felt lighter after my retirement from Corrections. This gave me more time to spend with my wife and attend to the concerns of the congregation. It forced me to think about the 5-year plans of the church. One of my members was a realtor who gave me a list of all the persons who lived within a one-mile radius. We did a small-scale evangelistic survey and found out that 90% of the people in the community were Buddhist. I sensed that was the case because most of the people receiving food on Wednesdays spoke Mandarin. Because of the language barrier, they never showed up for Worship Service or Bible study. Further research revealed once a Buddhist, always a Buddhist. The Food Bank program was supposed to be an evangelistic outreach, but not one person during my ministry at COAF came to church from the food distribution. This made me curious about what was happening on the Food Committee. I became more curious because every time I asked to go with them, I was rebuffed. Their attitude made me even more curious.

Chapter Thirty

Beware of Stiff-Necked People

"Beware of false prophets, who come to you in sheep's cloth-
ing, but inwardly they are ravenous wolves."
Matthew 7:15

For once, I want to tell the truth about a disobedient spirit in the church. From 2002 to 2008, I pastored the Church of All Faiths. One month before accepting this pastorate, I wrote a letter but never sent it prior to the interview. In the letter, I said I did not want to pastor this church. One of the reasons for not sending the letter was that I still believed this church had killed my father. Dad never shared his concerns, but I'm sure his brain cancer and ultimate death were related to the chronic stress he experienced with these church members.

The disobedient spirit was clear. One of the symptoms was not only how they shorted the church financially but also sought control. They wanted power and representation without accountability. The congregants thought they knew more about servant leadership than the pastor. They wanted people to follow them, but they were unwilling to follow me, whom they'd chosen as a leader. From a biblical perspective, they were like the mother of Zebedee's sons who asked Jesus, "Grant that these two sons of mine may sit, on Your right hand and the other on the left, in your Kingdom" (Mark 9:37). These disciples were so enamored of power, they could not see how humility was needed to lead people. Without Bible study, people are prone to errors of the flesh. This causes foolish mistakes that indicate individuals do not correctly understand the Word of God.

One thing I dislike is hypocrites. Jesus was emphatic about the temptation and danger of hypocrisy in scripture. People can appear clean on the outside, but inside, their hearts are dirty. At the Church of All Faiths, there was an insubordinate remnant. Sadly, this remnant thought I was blind! These individuals upset me because they seemed oblivious to the harm they were causing. They had no awareness of the effects of their behavior. Every time they entered a room, they would kill the spirit among the faithful gathered there. No scripture, preaching, Bible study, or truth would change their behavior.

They rarely tithed or gave more than ten dollars a month in the offering plate, but they fussed and cussed like major donors. This inequity really "chapped my hide" because it mirrored the hypocrisy Jesus spoke about.

To exacerbate the situation, these wayward people hung together. They sat in the same pews on the right side every Sunday. They balked about the same issues and were sticklers at every turn. These troublesome people caused stress among believing people who were trying to do the right thing. They were sneaky and deceptive, expecting no one to notice their double-minded tactics. But the treacherous breadcrumbs were all over.

Some of their breadcrumbs showed up in the food distribution program. Every week, the Food Committee received food from the Food Bank and distributed it. As a pastor, I noticed many of the defiant individuals were members of the Food Committee. I also noticed that every time I said, "I want to go to the Food Bank," the committee leadership balked at my request. When this happened consistently, I knew something illegal was going on.

The day I eventually went to the Food Bank, I rode in the passenger seat. I saw how our team selected the best items and brought them back for distribution. I also saw them consulting each other about getting the best selections. They ensured the members of the Committee got the finest quality products right off the top. They even had the gall to offer me Grade A items! They appeared to have no awareness that what they were doing was wrong. There was no mindfulness about connecting ministry or evangelism with distributing food to the poor. It was one thing to speculate about what they were doing but another to see it.

Going there helped me understand at a deeper level why new spiritual ideas were never accepted by these people. They resisted the movement of the Holy Spirit in the church and put up obstacles to every positive move related to choir, children's ministry, and leadership ideas. These fair-weather Christians attended church only when they could pontificate about their displeasures. In the process, they disrespected me, my wife, and my family. The worst example of this resistance was their blocking the decision to sell the church. Though the Steward Board and the church board had approved the sale, this disobedient remnant stood in the way with self-righteous words. Their Pharisaic actions rendered their membership insignificant because they vehemently opposed the desires of the Church Conference and the by-laws of the Church. Their behavior was so obstinate that I had to send a "Cease and Desist" letter to some of them. Dealing with them reminded me of the parable about letting the wheat and the tares grow together. This was the most difficult part of my ministry, and in the end, this group's disobedience caused me to resign.

I believe that my decision to sell the church was the right thing to do, which was confirmed years later when the same group of disobedient individuals asked me to come back and lead them in a church drive to move to another location.

Though I do not know for sure, I got an inkling in those six years of the headaches Dad experienced pastoring these stiff-necked people. I protected my heart and spirit against any entanglement they wanted to involve me in. Though my heart forgives them, I still feel the pain of their arrows when I am in their presence. Thank God for the transforming power of Jesus that can wash away all transgressions. I'm glad I gained new wisdom dealing with this disobedient pack of wolves.

Not only was I confronted by the wolf pack and their attempts to discourage our progressive moves in public, but I was also attacked in private ways. One night on a Wednesday, a woman I'll call "Big Bosom Betty" came into the office. I arrived at 6:00 p.m., my usual time, to prepare myself for Prayer and Bible Study at 7:00 p.m. Big Bosom Betty arrived at the office to discuss how she was rearing her sons and daughters. This seemed appropriate enough since she had invited Susan and me over to her house for a delicious home-cooked meal. During Big Bosom Betty's earlier visits, she had mentioned that she had ministers and pastors in her family. When she said, "I've known a lot of pastors," I didn't think she was using the word in the Biblical sense. I just assumed she had acquaintances with ministers.

This evening, Big Bosom appeared to be extra friendly. My back was partially turned when she got up from her seat ten feet away. She mentioned that I looked tense typing at the computer and needed a neck rub.

I said, "That was alright."

Then she said, "I need to talk to you privately in your office."

Being alert but careful, I went to the office to listen to her concerns. As we sat in two chairs facing one another, Betty asked if I wanted to kiss her bosoms.

She said, "I know you don't get to touch or fondle a bosom like mine."

I told her, "Your behavior is inappropriate. I'm satisfied with my wife."

I immediately got up and escorted her out of the door, and said, "I will see you in Bible Study." After that night, I never saw Big Bosom Betty or her sons again. I guess the point of her membership at the church was to lure the pastor. I'm glad I had my armor on tight that night.

Since we're on the topic of inappropriate behavior, there was another woman who called me only around midnight. Because I was a pastor, I never knew if members were calling for prayer or some other assistance. I was always available to give prayer and encouragement to any member. This member, who I'll call "Midnight Creeper," often called me in the wee hours of the night. It generally appeared she had been drinking because no one in their right mind would call someone late just to chat. She always called to discuss ideas about the church. She felt because she had been the secretary of the church for years, she had special access. I listened to her suggestions and assured her we were trying to make changes. I usually got her off the phone by encouraging her to speak with her husband about these issues.

After much prayer and fasting, I decided to resign. The stress from the wolf pack, the legal issues, and church member harassment made this decision easy.

Chapter Thirty-One

A Dream Come True

"But you be watchful in all things, endure afflictions, do the work of an evangelist, fulfill your ministry."
2 Timothy 4:5

After my decision to resign, protocol demanded I take this issue to the Church Conference. I began, "With much prayer and trepidation, I have come tonight to resign. Challenging situations at the church have led me to believe the growth of this church would be better served with someone else at the helm."

I explained my reasons and gave the church two weeks' notice. I had given the Church of All Faiths six years and three months of blood, sweat, and tears against my better judgment. It was time to put my ministerial talents to good use in another pasture.

One redeeming postscript occurs to me as I reflect on the six-year Church of All Faiths experience. If my Mom had any ill feelings about my life, my ministry resolved those issues through preaching, teaching, prayers, and pastoral care. I took this assignment because of Mom, and I prayed my efforts would help Mom heal from Dad's death. In the end, she could not even stomach the disrespect of the wolf pack. I gave everything despite the hostile environment. The day after my official resignation, I called the Navy Reserve Detailer and let them know my availability for mobilization anywhere in the world.

The Detailer said, "I have a location in San Diego, working at the Navy Mobilization site."

"Sign me up," I said. "I'm ready."

The Detailer gave me a start date of August 26th, 2008, to give me a chance to get my affairs in order. If COAF was the worst of times, Navy mobilization was the best of times. My wife was relieved I was getting away from the heathens and knew I needed to decompress from six years of hell. With uniforms, gear, and personal belongings in hand, I headed to my pre-stage site at Port Hueneme, CA. After being examined by the physician, I drove to my mobilization site in San Diego.

That mobilization had taken fifteen years to manifest. It was difficult to quit my job with the prison, though I knew legally the position was guaranteed. I didn't want to be away from the children in case they needed me. But this dream of mobilization had been present ever since my childhood in Louisiana. Every time I saw the gunshot wound on my father's right triceps, I wanted to understand the wounds of war. I never viewed myself as a combatant, but I wanted to experience the internal wounds of the heart. So many were traumatized; I wanted to understand PTSD. I always imagined myself playing an instrument in the military band as the troops came back from deployment. Now, as a chaplain, I was able to pray and bring others into God's orchestra. My purpose was to encourage soldiers to hear God's voice and listen to His still, small voice of assurance.

I checked into the mobilization site and was told my living quarters would be at the Coronado Base. I was excited to drive across the bridge, knowing every morning I would be driving across this bridge to work. The first night, I drove down to the beach five minutes away, put on my sand shoes, walked to the water, and thanked God for bringing me through the trials of the Church of All Faiths. Though I was staying in bachelor quarters, I sold Susan on the idea of visiting me. I encouraged her to fly down and have long walks on the beach, shop at the

Fashion Valley Mall, and enjoy as many sunsets as her soul could hold.

I loved this new schedule. Every week, I got the opportunity to teach a Combat Operational Stress Continuum class. I was teaching people how to assess their individual levels of stress as well as the collective stress of their teams and how to be proactive instead of reactive in high-stress situations. The class totaled fifty to three hundred soldiers preparing to participate in Operation Iraqi Freedom. Along with a new group of troops every week, I also ministered to the fifty reservists who were part of the Navy Mobilization staff.

My second command responsibility was taking care of another set of staff and the hundred soldiers who were assigned to Med Hold, people who had returned on medical leave and were unable yet to return home. I felt useful and appreciated. My energy was enhanced as I worked out daily from 11 a.m. to 1 p.m. I'm glad the military takes physical training seriously. This was the motivational schedule I had wanted all my life. I woke up every morning singing, "This is the day the Lord has made" (Psalm 118:124). Every time I went to the gym at 11 a.m., I sang, "Let everything that hath breath praise the Lord" (Psalm 150), and every night before bed, I sang, "Bless the Lord, O my soul, and all that is within me bless His Holy Name" (Psalm 103). To use a cliché often heard in San Diego, "I was living the dream."

I went into this experience with the words of Jesus firmly settled in my spirit. Especially Matthew 10:16: "Behold I send you out as sheep in the midst of wolves. Therefore, be wise as serpents and harmless as doves." I realized the labor I was undertaking could be overwhelming. I also knew there might be a degree of mental, physical, and emotional suffering. I knew I would face wicked people and demons that would try to oppose me.

Most of my suffering came from one person, the XO—the executive officer, who was second in charge. I'll call her CDR Highway. That's how it felt because everything had to be done according to her standards, even though the action might not be right. I had to stay as far away as possible from this person.

CDR Highway would say things like, "We don't do things that way, Chaplain, you need to read the Command rules."

I would say very cordially, "Thank you, XO," but under my breath, I was perturbed.

It wasn't that I minded being instructed, but there is a way to give instructions to people who are of the same rank. During the fifteen years I had served as an officer, there was mutual respect. No one before this mobilization had spoken down to me or demeaned me. I never let her see me sweat because that would jeopardize the interaction.

Most commands do not understand the job of the Chaplain, and many make policy on the spot because they do not want to appear ignorant. I let James 1:19 guide my daily interaction: "Wherefore, my beloved brethren, let every man be swift to hear, slow to speak." I would first listen to the words that were directed at me, then I would respond. Sometimes, I would speak, and other times, I would observe and chronicle a possible response for future interactions. Every day was a learning experience, but our schedule was based on a new set of mobilizing soldiers arriving weekly.

The question for me was how to get involved in the command in a plausible way every week. I found new ways to implement pastoral care skills. My Med Hold group asked me to lead them in prayer for morning muster. I became the Command Financial Officer for my unit because I had a Bachelor of Science degree in Business Management and Agricultural Economics. With this responsibility, I counseled my staff in money management and encouraged fiscal responsibility for those being deployed. Some soldiers had left their families without a budget, so I had to intervene and do family counseling in the four days I had with them before deployment.

On the medical side, when a soldier's blood pressure was high, I developed a method to lower pressure by 30 points in 15 minutes. I would sit down and listen to the soldier's anxiety and then lead them into a period of meditation accompanied by slow music. Every candidate who was given to me to lower their blood pressure passed. There were moving parts and pieces, but the key was thinking and praying on my feet.

One of the true joys of serving as the Command Chaplain was the interdisciplinary meetings with Med Hold staff on Tuesday mornings. Though I didn't have the training yet as a Clinical Chaplain who could advise on the total well-being of soldiers in care, the psychiatrist, psychologist, and licensed social worker appreciated my input. This is where I developed the desire to pursue clinical training. I challenged myself to be the best. I was driven to let other Navy personnel know, just because I was at least ten years older, that I was going to exceed my own expectations. I ran in every 5-mile race and participated in every physical fitness challenge.

I not only wanted to show my talents at my Command, but I also looked for other opportunities in the Region. I was chosen to say prayers at both the Ronald Reagan and Richard Nixon Libraries. Though I never considered myself political, I thought if I went the extra mile, I might get a higher point for leadership on my annual FITNESS reports. Whenever no one was available to do a baptism on a ship, a funeral service, or a wedding, I made myself available. The Command realized that they didn't own me exclusively: I was also supervised by Navy Region Southwest. This Command was not going to write my narrative; I was determined to write my own story.

Part of writing that narrative was participating in the political moment in America. In November, Barack Obama was elected as the 44th President of the United States. That was a day that I thought I would never see. My father and I had been involved in Voter Registration all our lives. The election of President Obama seemed like the blessing of all our hard work. I felt an additional blessing because Pres. Obama's father is from Kenya. My 2.5 years in the Peace Corps in Kenya gave me a deeper sense of connection to him.

One of the concerns that I thought would be a problem was getting time off to go to the inauguration. Though I had served only four months on mobilization, my wife and older sister felt it was imperative that we attend. Fortunately, we had cousins who lived in the District of Columbia area with whom we could stay. Since we were going back in the winter, we prepared ourselves for the elements.

On the day of the inauguration, Tuesday, January 20th, 2009, we got up at three a.m. so we could take the Metro at four a.m. I could not believe the crowds. The sheer number was massive. With this density, it was imperative to grab your loved one's hand if you wanted to maintain a connection. When we got to our Metro stop, it felt like we were being pushed by a tsunami wave of bodies. I have never experienced this in my life. We piled out of the train and headed to line up in the 37-degree cold. The line was slow, but at least it moved. After two hours, we found a place to sit where we could see the stage and the large 75-inch monitors that were placed on the sides.

One of the highlights of Pres. Obama's first inauguration was when Aretha Franklin sang, "My County, 'Tis of Thee." I had played this song at least 100 times, marching with the Weldonian Marching Band and other school bands. This song had never sounded as sweet as on this historic day. As I stood and listened, tears rolled down my cheeks for all the people in my generational family who had felt the whip of the slave master upon their backs. I cried for my grandfather, who could not go to school because it was against the law in Louisiana. For the persecution my father had received in the U.S. Army and the difficulties he faced in the Civil Rights struggle. The tears warmed my face as the words from Obama's lips warmed our hearts. It was a proud day to be an American, and I felt further joy being an officer serving under this honorable President.

Not only was the inauguration a historic day, but leaving the airport also proved to be eventful. As we entered the airport, I looked over and saw LL Cool J giving an empowering speech to a small gathering.

I went up to his bodyguard and asked, "Could I take a picture with Cool J after his speech?"

The guard said, "Okay." So, I moseyed over to Cool J and asked, "Can I take a selfie with you?"

He said, "Sure," stood next to me, and smiled. That picture became the most popular picture on my Navy office desk. Often, I would come back to the Chaplain's office, and the picture was gone, but fortunately, someone would eventually return it. I am grateful that the Command gave me the opportunity to experience this historic moment.

One of the blessings of having two commands was that I could pick and choose which Command was more flexible as I followed my ministry goals. It is common for liturgical Protestants and Catholics to have Ash Wednesday ceremonies, so I chose to use Med Hold for Ash Wednesday services. It was exciting to have at least 30 people participate in a weekday service. It was my first religious program. I was encouraged by the turnout of those who came from the two commands and others in the area.

Though we worked six out of seven days, the Mobilization Command was understanding concerning important family events. In May 2009, my middle daughter Naivasha graduated from the University of Las Vegas in Theater Design. I was not sure what she was going to do with her degree, but I knew it would be impactful and creative. I always let Naivasha know she had the drive and the intelligence to do whatever she wanted.

It was a blended gathering with my oldest daughter, Alecia, her husband, Dewellyn, and her two daughters. Mom attended as I paid her way, and my youngest daughter Kayla was there, along with several of Naivasha's friends. It was one of the few times when all my daughters were together, so I was able to take a picture with them. I treasure that weekend.

An important decision that summer was asking the Command to allow me to be a Chaplain Intern at Sharp Metropolitan Hospital. That meant leaving early one day a week so I could improve my skills. This Clinical Pastoral Education (CPE) opportunity was the most significant endeavor in my career to date. It enhanced my Navy career and prepared me for choice opportunities after Navy retirement.

Chapter Thirty-Two

Never Enough

"So then, my beloved brethren, let every man be swift to hear,
slow to speak, slow to wrath."
James 1:19

One of the blessings of the Clinical Pastoral Education (CPE) program was learning how to do a "verbatim"—observing the patient, my feelings, and the pastoral plan before I even engaged a patient. The hospital and the Command were my main emphases during this seven-month internship.

When I started the CPE program in July 2009, my world changed. My spiritual eyes opened to a new way of assessing people. I leaned into a holistic and spiritual evaluation of every experience. I developed more empathy for CDR Highway. I listened to her tone of voice, observed her walk, and noticed how she responded to stress. As I observed my own weaknesses, I began to see vulnerabilities in others. I never shared this information with CDR Highway, but my heart changed when I was in her presence.

As I listened to her explain Command problems, I noticed she justified her actions. She said, "I had to do what I did, or the Command would be jeopardized."

I considered whether her words matched her body language. More mature now, I did not run from CDR Highway as I had in the past. I remembered when I had positioned myself at the opposite end of the hallway when she approached. We should never run and hide from the people we work with. As I raised my awareness, I realized many of the enlisted staff were traumatized by her leadership.

As I walked among the workspaces and cubicles during the day, I saw sad faces. I heard enlisted staff say, "Chaplain, if you only knew."

When I asked, "Do you want to talk?" tears welled in their eyes. If they said, "Not now," I gave them my card.

The staff wore their feelings on their sleeves. They knew I knew! The oppression and abuse they were going through were thick in the atmosphere. They saw it happen to me, so they knew the abuse was not isolated. She treated officers in an equally caustic manner. When they saw that, they established a code language. I managed to establish a rapport with them, which was unusual between officers and enlisted personnel. They had a language, and their trust in me helped me understand their pain at a deeper level. I slept better, knowing that my mobilization experience was evolving.

My experience with CDR Highway also evolved. She shared insider notes without knowing that the enlisted staff trusted me. I intuited the XO's personal concerns and tried to understand her humor. As a result, she included me more in leadership discussions. That slight change lowered my blood pressure and anxiety.

One day, the XO called me into her office to say, "You know what's happening with BM3 Murphy." I nodded and waited for her to explain more. I never let on what I knew when she began to confide about one case or another. I never wanted to show my hand.

It was exciting to be part of a Command where I was involved in people's lives. I was moving with the Op tempo. Though it took six months, my spirit was lifted when I was finally included in weekly preparation briefs. The briefs indicated when staff or the mobilized were 'low-hanging fruit'—physically, mentally, or emotionally unready for mobilization. If I listened, the executive staff laid the tracks for my daily encounters. With the trust of the inner circle, I was finally being used effectively. My Command referred hard cases to me for assessment. Daily, I thought my presence was strategically important and appreciated.

As a reservist for fifteen years prior to being mobilized, I had shown up once a month. During that period, the executive command decisions were never vetted through me. Being mobilized, I finally experienced what it meant to be an integral part of people's lives. I worked with other mobilized Reservists, and we operated cohesively as a Unit.

A more secure status with the Mobilization Command enhanced my expertise with the MED Hold Command. Because the expectations in the CPE program were high, my desire to serve those with medical issues increased. I asked returning soldiers if they were having PTSD concerns, particularly sleeplessness and anxiety. I visited the hospital to see if soldiers had appointments at midnight and understood fully what it meant to be a 24/7 chaplain. The high ideals of the CPE program helped me understand this ministry of presence.

Because there were no roadblocks at the top of the hierarchy, MED Hold gave me more freedom to deal with clinical issues. Every soldier I met was either mobilizing to Iraq or returning from being down-range. Even if they were not assigned to me officially, they became my patients. I never called them patients, but That's how they were treated as returning soldiers who continued to heal in mind, body, and spirit. My goal was to return them to a place of normalcy. My presence eased the anxiety of having to see doctors, psychiatrists, and psychologists who were not always user-friendly. I relished the opportunity to be part of their recovery.

I loved the benefits of Med Hold. Several organizations con-
tributed funds that allowed this Command to attend San Diego
Padres and San Diego Chargers games. I appreciated the fellowship and camaraderie of this distinguished community. We
had an ethical and moral code of honor, courage, and commitment. When any of us saw the other person straying from the
moral code, we addressed that person privately. There was
more esprit de corps from this military environment than I had
ever seen in the church. I often thought I had to be mobilized
in the military to understand what it means to experience *koi-
nonia*. This is the Greek word for fellowship. I understand now
why the Apostle Paul used military metaphors. Everybody in
Paul's times knew how the military treated them, so they were
familiar with his illustrations.

Towards the end of the summer of 2009, I asked my mother
to come down with her best friend, Doris. I paid for her plane
flight, hotel room, and expenses while she was in San Diego. I
enjoyed treating Mom to the life I had been wanting to live
since joining the military. I knew Mom based her life and evaluation of people on money. I was blessed to join her on a bus
tour of San Diego and bought her and her friend a $75 brunch
at Hotel Coronado.

While she visited, Mom said, "You've made it."

I asked, "What does that mean?"

She said, "Well, it appears that you've found your calling."

"Mom, I have been in my calling since I was ordained in
1982. This is just another form of that calling. It appears no
matter what ministry I am involved with, it's never enough for
you!"

Mom went silent. She often became quiet when I caught her
in a calculated denial of my personhood. She didn't realize
every time she brought up my calling, she demeaned my vocational efforts. She belittled my twelve years of pastoring,
twenty years of prison ministry, and up to that point, fifteen

years of a military career. Her lack of nurture has been the thorn in my flesh. It's a pain that would never be resolved, so I lived with this long-suffering. Mom celebrated mammon over stewardship. Her comment was typical of her double standard. I believe paying her way to San Diego made a difference in her perception of me. I never expected love, appreciation, or financial help from Mom. Because Dad worked with Dr. Rev. Martin Luther King, Jr., I wanted to go to Morehouse. My parents, especially Mom, didn't share that hope. As I got to know Mom's history with her dad, I felt she punished me for what she didn't receive from her parents. I never felt Mom understood my career intentions. But I was glad she saw how happy I was in my mobilized command.

Family visits enhanced and normalized my time in San Diego. When Susan's older sister Judie visited from Virginia with her husband Rickey, we were a joyful foursome. They stayed in the same living quarters area on Coronado Base, went to Balboa Park for Christmas, and attended a football game between the Chargers and their favorite team, the Dallas Cowboys. Even my younger sister Kelesha and husband Wayne dropped by to enjoy the San Diego area.

The best visits were with my daughters. I especially appreciated Naivasha's visits because her schedule was hectic, and she couldn't come often. The area was familiar to her because she had spent time in the Community College there. My love for Naivasha was special because I was forced to separate from Angel, her mother, at a critical time in her young life. I always felt we were playing catch up for the lost moments caused by separation and divorce.

I also felt a closeness to my daughter Kayla because we seemed to understand each other. I visited her at Biola, where she was an undergrad. As a result of the mobilization, the military gave me aid, which allowed me to help Kayla with her schooling. I enjoyed traveling to Orange County, going to church with her, and spending time at Huntington Beach. I loved praising God and talking about the sermon afterward. And I loved it when Kayla was able to visit me in San Diego. We went to the beach and Carlsbad, which became one of her favorite cities.

The work was good. Life was good. At this season of my life, I felt I had become a center of gravity for my family and friends. They all took time in their busy schedules to touch base with me as they continued to grow, and I grew with them.

Chapter Thirty-Three

Surrounded by Trauma

"Come unto Me, all you who labor and are heavy laden, and I will give you rest."
Matthew 11:28

During the day-to-day Command operations, I was grateful that the Navy honored grief. In September 2009, Aunt Glen died. My mother asked me to attend and assist with the funeral services in Louisiana. It was an honor to wear my military uniform in the presence of my blood relatives. My Louisiana family on both sides had strong patriotic commitments. Mother believed my presence might inspire Aunt Glen's grandsons.

It was enlightening to see how family members grieved. The relative who was most affected was Aunt Geneva, my Uncle Walter's wife. Geneva's usual disposition was smiling and other-centered. She epitomized Southern hospitality. When I got off the plane from San Diego, she showered me with care.

"Robert, can I get you anything? Did you eat anything on the plane?"

"No, Geneva, I'm good, maybe later when I settle in."

"Don't hesitate. You know Aunt Geneva will do what I can to make your time pleasant."

"I know, Aunt Geneva. Just give me a firm bed and some soul food, and I'll be set."

She was her usual loving self, except on the day of the funeral. Grief appeared to bring out the dual side of love. If you love deeply, you will grieve deeply. Of all the relatives, Geneva's face was saddest. I can only speculate why. I believe Geneva had a close relationship with Glen, which made her feel she had lost more than a friend. Both Geneva and Glen had spent most of their life in the Lafayette/Martinsville area. Though Geneva had no children of her own, she sympathized with Glen's rearing of her children and grandchildren. Glen and Geneva spent weekends and holidays sharing family responsibilities. Geneva lost more than a sister-in-law; she lost her prayer partner and confidante. Glen's passing was a deep emotional wound for her.

Family members who were not as close appeared a bit more lighthearted during the funeral. One of the saddest facts about Glen's death was that she was younger than Mom by ten years. Given her sisters' longevity, Aunt Glen seemed to have died before her time. When people die prematurely, hearts and minds work overtime to find a reason. Glen had been divorced from the father of her children for twenty years. The responsibility of raising children as a single parent was challenging. Also, everybody had questions about the boyfriend she had befriended for years but never married. All the rumors and secrets that had been hidden in emotional closets came out. My CPE training prompted me to want to stay another month to listen to these family concerns. I wanted to ensure that generational trauma would not be transferred to the grandchildren. Because they lived two thousand miles away, I didn't know if I would ever see them again. But I had to leave them in God's hands. I left confident that God would heal and direct their paths.

After returning to San Diego, Susan and I planned a three-day vacation to Mexico. This was a benefit of being stationed near the border: quick get-a-way opportunities. I learned at the depth of the counseling process that self-care was critical for restoration. Though it was a short cruise, this gave me time to decompress from Aunt Glen's passing. I was grateful it didn't take much prodding to get Susan to go on an adventure. We loved quality time together. We decided to visit the blowhole at La Bufadora. This blowhole is famous because it shoots further than any of the others in the world. We had seen the blow hole near Sandy Beach, Oahu, and the one near Lahaina, but this one was substantially higher.

Returning refreshed, I continued with weekly CPE training and reflected on the impact of this training. I believe CPE training put me into a season of heightened cautiousness. In CPE group work, I feared saying or doing something that would be perceived as inappropriate. I never liked explaining myself to anyone. I didn't want to put myself in a position of being defensive, so I worked hard not to offend others. This concern with not wanting to be offensive created a habit of double-thinking. I recycled things in my mind, thoughts, and heart. I prayed about words before they ever came out of my mouth because once I said them, I could not take them back. I kept Proverbs 23:7 on the tip of my tongue: "For as a man thinks in his heart, so is he."

Hospital training dovetailed with military life. One of the things we were required to do in CPE training was a "verbatim" report on patient visits. As soon as I returned to San Diego, I visited a Caucasian woman around fifty with bradycardia weakness during my CPE rounds and did a verbatim on her. The room was well-lit with sunlight, and the time was around 10 a.m. The patient was wearing a blue hospital gown, a tennis shoe on her left foot, and a walking boot on her right foot.

(To patient) "May I come in?"

"Yes, (patient gathers pillows and blankets) I've got to move this stuff that my son used."

"Did your son stay last night?"

"Yes, he did. I wish you could meet him. How are you?"

"I'm fine. I'm Chaplain Jerome, and I'm here to visit you."

"I'm here with an irregular heartbeat. I came in last night, and the staff is determining my situation. I'm a PK (preacher's kid), and I just moved here from Texas in June."

(For clarification) "June of this year?"

"Yes, June of this year. I moved here to be close to my son, who is in the Navy. My uncle was also in the service as a chaplain. He died at the end of WWII. He was a good man. I have a lot of family that have died during the past five years. My younger brother died in 2004; my sister died in 2005; my dad died in 2007; my husband died in January of this year. (Tears welled up in the patient's eyes as she reached out to touch my hands). So much has happened during the past five years. I was diagnosed with muscular dystrophy in 2005. That's when I decided to stop driving. I said to myself that I was not going to be the cause of someone dying as a result of my muscular dystrophy."

"How has that been…not driving?"

"You never realize how much you drive until you stop driving. I used to help people out, taking them all over the place."

(Since the patient said she was a PK, I asked if she had a church family) "Do you have a church home?"

"No."

"Would you like me to bring you a list of churches?"

"Yes."

"Any particular faith denomination?"

"My folks were Church of God, but I am not choosy as long as the Word is being preached and people are loving."

"I'll bring a church list after lunch."

(Then the patient's son walked in, and delight and gratitude seemed to come over her. The patient introduced me, and I subtly indicated I was in the Navy.)

"Would you like to pray?"

"Yes." (The son stood, and the patient, too, but I suggested she sit because her right foot was broken. I also sat.)

"Lord, bring healing to my sister in Christ's foot and normalcy of heartbeat. We thank you for the medical staff and this son for his continued support."

"May I have one of your cards?"

"Let me go get one. I'll be right back." (I walked back to the office and returned.)

"Here's my card and a church list."

(The patient asked for a card for her son, who had just returned from Iraq.) I believe my son is experiencing some PTSD but doesn't want to own up to the fact that he needs any help."

In reflection, the ease that the patient showed and the meeting of the son made this a complete visit for the first time. You rarely get to meet the patient's family members or advocates. My desire to listen to the entire story made the patient and her son want to disclose critical pieces of their life narrative.

The connections between the two parts of my professional life ran deep. As I listened to issues related to PTSD in the hospital and went to bed, I realized more PTSD stories would be waiting for me at my MED Hold Command.

Chapter Thirty-Four

Everything Comes to an End

"Being confident of this very thing, that He who has begun a good work in you will complete it until the day of Jesus Christ."
Phil. 1:6

I've mentioned that CPE training heightened my tendency to be cautious. At the military command, I was seen as the executive leadership. At the hospital, I was a lowly Chaplain Intern at the bottom of the hospital totem pole, but that position humbled me.

In a servant's role there, I was discreet in my actions. I watched my language and manners and was prudent about what I said to a patient. I had to put my ego at the door and shed some of the habits of leadership. No one here cared about my rank. It was not my job here to take charge. I did not want to give offense. I walked a fine line between speaking my truth and being diplomatic. Because we wrote verbatim, I tried to ensure my conversations with patients did not adversely affect the group evaluations.

What I desired was fluidity. I wanted the Holy Spirit to lead rather than being rule-bound. I listened to music between my counseling sessions to decompress and maintain balance in my evaluations. It cleared my spirit so I wouldn't take the last patient's tensions into the next visit. Music has a beginning, middle, and end. I used that analogy in my active listening process. Though it was tedious, I wanted to take the CPE process to the end of the road—a full four units. Each unit involved 400 hours of counseling. Still, I looked forward to each precious hour of discovery.

With each weekly "didactic," a required instructional time, new paths of vulnerability were opened. Writing helped me be receptive to opinions and perspectives. In the desire to be transparent, I acknowledged stumbling blocks and detours I might encounter.

In 2010, I realized the end of my mobilization was imminent. I was on my last set of extended orders, desperately trying to hold out for more time. I wanted more Active Duty. I wanted to hold on to this military world, this ideal schedule of work, exercise, and execution. The life I had waited fifteen years for was coming to an end. This was a transition I dreaded.

But mobilization, much as I enjoyed it, had to end. I had an opportunity to extend, but in an interview with another Command, I opened my mouth when I should have kept it shut. The Commanding Officer asked me about extra duty, and I said, "I was fine as long as I didn't have to work seven days straight." That didn't sit well with the interviewing commanding officer. On reflection, CPE training has taught me about self-care. For over two years, I had worked six days a week, and I did not want to continue that type of op tempo. It was time for me to write my own military narrative.

In the end, "all things worked together for good." If I had taken the job I was pursuing, I would not have liked being supervised by a dictator, which seemed likely. I might not have liked being supervised by someone who did not understand African-American leadership, which he didn't. I did not want to repeat another chapter of CDR Highway. A horrible relationship with a commanding officer would have overshadowed the two and a half years of what seemed like an ideal situation and lessened my high Fitness Reports.

I dreaded going back home to civilized life. I had no desire to pastor or work in a prison. This transition seemed as though it would be a little like mandatory sleep. There are times we don't want to slumber, but we must, for restoration. I was fighting this change at two levels. One, I didn't want mobilization to end, and two, I didn't want to start another transition. I didn't know what the change would look like. Everything I was doing to prepare for it didn't work—nothing that I applied for came through—so I entered another intentional faith walk.

This was the difficult part of my journey. My planned life was going to turn into an unplanned life in which I felt like I had no control. Nothing I tried to do came to fruition. My work in the period of mobilization had come to perfect fruition, but in transition, it looked as though life was falling apart.

Speaking with one of my fellow comrades, JB, who became my friend, eased the transition.

During our excursions away from the command, I would ask JB, "What does ending mobilization feel like?"

JB said, "Terminating mobilization was both a blessing and a curse. If you wanted to get high marks on your Fitness Reports, it was important to be mobilized, but eventually, everybody had to go home." Listening to someone else reflect on this transition helped me understand the challenge and the pain.

I had to say goodbye. This was the first time I had to leave a job I didn't want to leave. I had to say goodbye to this incredible city, Command, and relationships I had massaged for years. Even the antagonists who had entered my life had become allies. This Command manifested everything that should take place in a two-year period of professional development and growth.

I spent two years smoothing the stone, gaining favor from people I thought I could never gain favor from, impacting people's lives. They were part of my pathos and ethos. They had become my moral fiber.

I did not know how I was going to live without the smiles of those I had come to love. The high-fives, fist bumps, and jokes had become part of my daily motivation. There was an esprit de corps that was undeniable.

I can understand why some people don't want a war to end. They become so acclimated to a routine that it seems right, especially in war. In wartime, we lean on all our faculties for survival. Our responses become automatic. We don't want to adapt, but we must.

This is the dilemma I was dealing with. Going to see physicians to get my disability assessed released me from the funk of transition. For almost two years, retired Sgt. Taylor had mentioned getting assessed before my mobilization ended. I was determined to get what I had coming. I went to at least four doctors to get my body assessed for disability. I went to the podiatrist, who noticed I had developed bunions and foot alterations from marching and carrying heavy packs. The doctors also determined I had developed hearing loss. I tried to get the service to rate my gout and diabetes, but they said, "The Navy didn't cause this." It took a year to get the results of 30% disability from Atlanta.

I loved to go to a nightclub called Humphrey's Backstage. Almost every Friday night during my mobilization, I headed there to dance. I usually met some dancing partners who loved to boogie. Whoever got to the venue first would hold the table for three other people. As I watched the musicians, I wanted to take the stage. Fortunately, the nightclub held a contest in September 2010. I asked my younger sister if she would come down and perform some songs we had practiced in the summer of 2008. Kelesha agreed, and we took the stage with Kelesha on clavinova and me on alto saxophone and congas. I invited my friends, and though I was nervous, I felt satisfied that I had manifested another dream on my bucket list.

One of the greatest celebrations was my going-away party in December 2010. The party was held at my favorite restaurant in Coronado. The place rearranged all the chairs, and the command brought my favorite foods. My wife came down and met all the people who had supported me, along with those who hadn't. Both the officers and enlisted showed up in a celebratory mood. I put in the paperwork for a citation, but politics prevented it from being approved.

After returning home, still on mobilization orders, there was one incident that caused me to hasten my transition. After doing a funeral service in Stockton, I was traveling along the crosstown freeway, and a car on the side was traveling uncomfortably slowly. To avoid the slow vehicle, I got off the freeway and applied my brakes, but because the brakes had just been serviced, I hit the left embankment. In the process, my car jumped 50 feet and ended up on the right embankment. The transmission fluid leaked out, and the car was totaled.

I didn't want to have a car accident, but the accident forced me to stop and think about the post-mobilization process. I looked at my body, my schedule, and my priorities. I had to slow down. That process meant that I had two agendas: one, trying to get into a CPE program, and two, teaching school to bring in more money. It was not an ideal situation, but it was a slower pace for a while to regroup until my dream job as a VA chaplain came through. In the words of Job, "I was going to wait until my change comes."

Chapter Thirty-Five

Inspired to Be the First

"Wisdom is the principal thing; Therefore get wisdom. And in all your getting, get understanding."
Proverbs 4:7

As a result of the accident, I had to buy a new car. I was grateful that the insurance company gave me a thousand dollars for the parts of my 2002 Land Rover. It was a great car, but the serviceman had said at the December 2010 tune-up that it was "time for a new car," so I didn't feel bad when it was totaled. With this accident, my life reached new heights of strange coincidences. I felt every unfolding consequence was a serendipitous experience.

I hated looking for a new car, particularly when I was pressed for time. I looked high and low and finally found a Flex-Fuel vehicle at an Enterprise lot. This was a frugal move, as Flex Fuel vehicles use 85% ethanol, which is one dollar cheaper than 87%. I bought a red Ford Escape because I loved the color. From an eschatological perspective, I figured when Jesus comes back, I'll be covered in the blood of the Lamb who died on the cross. That theological perspective helped to protect and calm me as I traveled.

The accident forced me to go to the VA clinic for a check-up on my back. The physical therapist (PT), Dave Eng, was very experienced. He gave me a hip flexor to wear every day, and eventually, I bought my own. Though I have run through six hip flexors, it has been the best protective device for my well-being. I wear it to ensure I maintain physical health. When I don't wear this hip flexor, I feel shooting pains down my right leg.

As I healed, I reached out to the Fairfield/Suisun City School District about substitute teaching. After I received an Emergency Permit, I would call each evening to hear what was available to teach the next day. I loved listening to the options. My priority was teaching English and Math. One of the joys of teaching was how I started every class. As I stood in front of the class with my double-breasted coat, more professional-looking than most of my colleagues, I engaged the students as they entered class.

When I saw one saggin'—showing their underwear—I told them, "Pull up your pants. Saggin's not allowed in my class-room."

As I saw young girls putting eyeliner on their eyes, I said, "Put your makeup away; you are beautiful just as you are."

After those directives, I gave a brief lesson on saggin'.

I asked the class, "Where do you think saggin' came from?"

The class said, "Prison."

I said, "Nope, I worked in prisons for twenty years, and in-mates were mandated to wear belts."

Somebody else yelled out, "Tommy Hilfiger."

I said, "Nope, they fooled you again. The real fact is the fashion world doesn't want you to know that saggin' came from slavery. The slave masters didn't give slaves belts intentionally to lower their self-esteem. Every time one of you walks around saggin', you are perpetuating the low-esteem mindset slave masters wanted slaves to have 150 years ago. Finally, what is saggin' spelled backward?" They hesitated. "Niggas." "That's intentional, and behind your back, That's what people will call you."

I posed another question directly to the girls: "Girls, would you marry any of these guys who sag?"

They all said, "No." "Then why do you give them the time of day? Girls, why do you put makeup on? Do you put it on because of peer pressure or because you think if you put it on, you'll get that special guy?"

"Guys, do you like natural beauty or painted beauty?" The guys unanimously said, "Natural beauty."

I loved my role as a substitute teacher for more than the opportunity to teach. I knew I was probably the first and only African-American male teacher they had ever had. I never had one during elementary and secondary school, but the need was great. By the time I started teaching, I had noticed that online African-American males received special educational and monetary incentives to teach in the inner city.

I told them, "I'm your captain now. I don't know what your teacher allows, but I'm your sheriff today." During my substitute days, if I knew where I was teaching, God would wake me up in the morning around 5 a.m. with a rap song for the school where I was going. I told the students that I didn't want to see my rap song on YouTube, so I discouraged them from recording me. At the end of class, I would ask for somebody to "spit for me" to create a rhythm. The following is an example of the rap songs that I prepared for Rodriguez High, entitled "Rodriguez High Challenge."

Intro
What's up, Mustangs? Time to challenge your view
And look at the world with the goals you pursue.

Chorus
Regardless of what your friends or parents say,
You are somebody with a duty today;
So, I charge you this moment

Admonish you now,
Don't let anybody determine your Wow;

Verse One
Because one day, Mom said I'd never finish tenth grade
In my early years, she was throwing some shade.
Dad said I was useless, could always be a pimp,
But that didn't help my emotional limp.

Verse Two
Because I've got mountains to climb and countries to cross,
One day, somebody is gonna call me a boss;
When the roll is called, and the muster is taken,
I'll tell the story everyone was mistaken;

Verse Three
Now, I hope you're listening and take this sonnet to heart,
Once you go down the wrong path, it's hard to restart;
Take it from this OG, and avoid the pain,
No one knows the catalyst inside your brain;

Tag
So, I charge you this moment
Admonish you now,
Don't let anybody determine your Wow;
Right now, determine your Wow,
In your heart, make a vow,
In your mind, you'll make it somehow,

I was fortunate to look like Barack Obama—same skin tone, same height, and ten pounds heavier. So, guys, particularly, called me "Obama" when they saw me enter the school grounds.

In response to my rap songs, one of the students in my English Honors class, John Luke Bruni, wrote a poem about me entitled "Poem for Mr. Thomas."

What I witnessed, I can't believe my eyes,
A truly majestic creature has fallen from the sky;
Never in my days did I anticipate such a teacher,
In this Greek-speaking, Kenyan teaching, God-fearing
preacher.

I have seen a lot of subs after many a sun and moon,
From timid Mr. Lionheart to Mr. Carl C. K. Koon,
I love Mr. Merrill, his respect goes off the grid,
But I have never heard him correctly pronounce the Hebrew
name Abed,
Yes, this man is something special; his style is very stellar,
Whenever he puts pen to paper, he writes a New York Best
Seller,
When he's not spinning gold, he moonlights at San Quentin,
It's rumored that he even converted Charles Manson into a
Christian.

He likes writing poetry, goes to high schools, and begins to
rhyme,
Has more flow than Easy E, Eminem, and Dr. Dre combined,
This man is a legend, no sub is quite the same,
So, I really cannot believe that no one knows his name.

I didn't write my songs for student response; I wrote them to relate and get the message across to the students about the importance of education. I tried to encourage them to stay in school. I told each class daily they had three choices in life: education, military, or prison, because if they didn't plan, then they planned to fail. I told them there wasn't anything romantic about being shot or getting stabbed. If you asked an inmate, they would rather be in the classroom than in the prison. I had to give them a reality check so they would take their education seriously.

In the midst of encouraging the students to stay in school, I continued to apply for CPE opportunities. Finally, late in November 2012, an opening became available at the Alta Bates Hospital in Berkeley. Interestingly, this was the same hospital where my first wife worked. I dropped her off and picked her up every day.

As we went into the interview, my second at Alta Bates, I tried to remember how I had answered before to ensure I didn't make the same mistake. I went over my answers and even traveled to Travis Air Force Base to get a professional interviewer to give me a mock interview. At the mock, we went over my answers. They encouraged me to take my time and answer the question but also amplify the answer if I had the opportunity. I followed their instructions, and one week after the CPE interview, I learned that I got the position and would be starting in January 2013 for less than five months. I felt privileged that after two years, I had finally gotten into my Unit Two class.

Chapter Thirty-Six

Vulnerability Can Be Painful

"For we wrestle not against flesh and blood, but against principalities, against powers, against the rulers of the darkness of this age, against spiritual hosts of wickedness in the heavenly places."
Ephesians 6:12

January 2012 brought immense joy as I started my second unit of Clinical Pastoral Education (CPE). I did not anticipate any problems, but once everybody introduced themselves, I knew this was going to be a time of spiritual warfare. The reason for my concern was the sexual orientation of the group.

I never considered myself to be a prejudiced person, but this was challenging. The first day of orientation was for initial introductions. As each CPE participant said their name, it was followed by a self-identifier such as bisexual or lesbian. When asked, I responded with my name but didn't identify my sexual orientation. I didn't feel it was necessary. The constant need to identify one's sexual orientation made me realize this was a unique CPE unit. The environment made me feel like I was surrounded by a group of sexually abused women. I was the only male. They never expressed it overtly, but there was an underlying tension in our conversation from the beginning. From that first day, I knew I had to walk gingerly. If I said the wrong word or exhibited body language they could misread, I would be perceived as insensitive to women's concerns.

I was aware of sexual injustices faced by women. Most of my girlfriends had experienced and talked about some form of sexual abuse. When I worked in the women's prison for sixteen years, I heard these stories daily. During my time in the military, women visited my office weekly to confide the sexual trauma they experienced from enlisted and senior leadership.

With the constant pressure to self-identify by sexual orientation, I felt demonic oppression. It showed up as abnormal fear. In a group where I was supposed to be free and vulnerable, I felt the opposite. Whatever the Bible said about gay and lesbian sexuality, I had to put those scriptures and feelings on pause. I did not want group time to be a forum for theological debate. I was fully aware that the effects of sexual assault are often "masked" by other feelings. Because people grieve differently, I did not want to open PTSD wounds. As a result, I tread lightly with my own feelings during this short five-month period. A negative evaluation from this second unit could have massive repercussions for my future units of CPE. My words might have caused trauma, which would be unforgivable by staff and colleagues. Another impact of this oppressive atmosphere was difficulty sleeping. Because my authenticity had to be held in check, I tossed and turned about how to be truthful. I prayed frequently "to have the tongue of the learned" and be quick to listen and slow to speak.

As I listened to the self-disclosures in the group, they sounded like individuals who had experienced abandonment. They discussed anxiety in relationships, feelings of worthlessness, and difficulty trusting others. The pain in this group dovetailed with the experiences I had heard from molested or traumatized women in the prison. My CPE group expressed similar feelings of isolation, loneliness, and not being accepted.

Listening to the trauma gave me greater empathy for the pain my colleagues were experiencing.

In my experience, addictions, dependencies, and escape were common ways victims processed abuse. So-called healthy people exhibited these behaviors when they tried to get relief from the torment of abandonment. People don't do drugs for no reason. Alcohol, cocaine, marijuana, and gambling, in my experience, are often alternative ways to deal with trauma.

Anger is a spirit that often exists because of the frustration of not being able to deal with life around abandonment. When one can't deal with issues by using drugs, anger often ensues.

Anxiety comes from the strongman of fear, which wears you out. Fear torments people, which causes them to be nervous, which leads to restlessness and weariness because they refuse to let go and let God. Jesus said, "Come unto me all ye that are heavy ladened, and I will give you rest" (Matthew 11:28-30).

I felt a spirit of depression in this group. One woman in the group discussed the challenges of being a woman in a man's world. She spoke of the difficulties of getting ordained and needing to earn approval from a male-dominated ministry. I knew through experience and research in the women's prison and military that homosexuals have one of the highest rates of suicide. A 2021 study by UCLA William Law Institute published in 2021 claimed, "More than 60% of suicide attempts among LGBQ people happen within five years of realizing they are LGBQ." I constantly felt as though I was on suicide watch, walking a tightrope of discernment. Related to bondage, scripture says, "Who the Son sets free is free indeed." If the Word doesn't lose you from the devices of the enemy, you are bound. Related to failure, scripture says, "The wages of sin is death." If you want to have success, the Bible says to meditate on the Word of God day and night.

The group talked about being transference-free, which is the shift of emotions from one person to another. However, I felt transference from my colleagues because I felt they were work-ing through their issues in the group. Their issues, which I felt prohibited from speaking about, often prevented my colleagues from being present and "showing up," emotionally available to the rest of us. I felt victimized, but I couldn't talk about this feeling because my masculine point of view would be suspect. The purpose of the CPE training was not a forum to psychoan-alyze each other; it was to learn how to do pastoral care in a hospital environment.

But I was frustrated that I couldn't be my authentic self, es-pecially with my three other colleagues. I couldn't talk about the fatigue I was experiencing, dealing with the anxiety about everyone's sexual orientation. I felt their heaviness of spirit, which caused compassion fatigue. If I said anything about my thoughts that they found objectionable, it would affect my weekly, mid-term, and final assessment. One misplaced word could cause a tsunami of hurt feelings. I didn't want the entire four months to be about me, so I kept quiet.

There were excellent moments of reflection during this challenging environment. Weekly, I met with my supervisor, whom I'll call Sallie. Sallie asked each week what I was feeling and what I was going through as a person. Every week we met, my heart was bursting to share all I had in "my well." In 2012, my well was full of decades of repressed, suppressed feelings. I felt I could release all this "stuff" with Sallie. I felt that if I was going to be the type of hospital chaplain who combined heart and head, I had to allow myself to be vulnerable, to be open and receptive to my vulnerability. This vulnerability was important for good pastoral care. I believe I had a synergistic relationship with Sallie. I believe there was nothing Sallie could not comprehend from an emotional perspective. She had the heart space and the intellectual acuity to listen and absorb all I was willing to divulge. I was moved to tears by Sallie's capac-ity to understand my heart. I felt blessed to know there was one person who understood the challenge of this season of CPE for me. Though she had a different sexual orientation, it was not a barrier between us. I accepted Sallie in all her humanity, and she accepted me. Ultimately, that was the blessing of this extended unit, learning to accept people in their unique humanity.

Lessons learned: there are seasons in your life when you must put your thoughts and feelings on hold. I believe the spiritual warfare I experienced from January to May was a training ground for future situations in the hospital environment. I believe we go through trials and tribulations for a season to prepare us for the future.

The On-Call experience during this unit was challenging. As interns, we were given pagers and had to sleep in the attic of the hospital for 48 hours. The combination of noise from the street and potential problems from two additional hospitals was stressful. Still, on March 2nd, 2012, I experienced the best On-Call I had ever experienced. I paced myself with appropriate breathing sessions throughout the weekend.

I met a particularly memorable patient during this On-Call. First, at 9 a.m., a 30-year-old oncology leukemia patient was in tears from severe pain. This patient was frustrated because she was receiving poor attention from nursing staff. After listening to her concerns, I had a conversation with the nurse. When I returned at 9 p.m., after the patient spent time with her family, medical attention had improved. After prayer, this same patient, who could not move because of the pain at 9 a.m., came walking out of the room with the IV stand in her right hand just to tell me, "Thank you, Chaplain." This was transformational for me and, hopefully, for the patient, family, and staff. It's amazing what agape love and concern can do for all parties involved. I believe in the scripture, "Hatred stirs up strife, But love covers all sins" (Proverbs 10:12).

Chapter Thirty-Seven

Create in Me a Clean Heart

"Be of the same mind toward one another. Do not set your mind on high things, but associate with the humble. Do not be wise in your own opinion."
Romans 12:16

The On-Call weekend of March 2nd provided the greatest dividend for spiritual growth. A woman whose unborn baby had died said she didn't want to talk to a chaplain, even after she requested the On-Call chaplain. The patient didn't want to talk to the chaplain Saturday morning, but after I spoke with my supervisor and received encouragement, I asked the nurse to ask her again. The third time, the patient said, "Yes," and I went into the room to provide at least a ministry of presence. This time, the patient asked questions about the grieving process. She said she didn't want to talk about the event but wanted to wait until she left the hospital. As I stood in her room silently praying, the patient revealed she had known something was wrong with her pregnancy from the first trimester. She talked about her intuitive awareness, even in the midst of her grief. I believe this patient's willingness to reflect on her experience was transformational. Her willingness to talk with me gave me confidence about the power of presence. This encounter re-moved a layer of fear about what to say in a sensitive situation. The patient did not want to talk about the loss of her unborn child, but by providing a ministry of presence, she was able to share her heart. She spoke more freely than I had ever experienced with a person in a similar stage of grief.

Since feedback from my colleagues was a growing part of my spiritual development, it was important to hear how I was being perceived. My supervisor, Sallie, made this evaluation of my pastoral work during the unit. "Robert reflected on his past experience being propositioned by men who have sex with other men and the fear that arose in him toward LGBTQ people as a result of this experience. This was a tender subject for Robert, and it took courage for him to bring this into individual supervision and dialogue with peers in mid-unit evaluations as well as Small Process Groups. Initially, Robert felt afraid to connect with his peer D, a lesbian woman married to another woman. He recognized this fear could prevent him from ministering effectively to LGBTQ persons and to his peers. Robert worked hard to distinguish his past experiences from his present experiences. He subsequently developed a strong and authentic working relationship with D and provided effective spiritual and emotional care to LGBTQ patients and staff."

The most rewarding comments I received from this extended CPE unit were the ones made by staff. An RN on the oncology floor wrote, "Robert brings an uplifting energy to the unit the moment he steps on the floor. If I am overwhelmed and visibly stressed, it literally takes a few sentences to bring a smile to my face, and his personality has been a great gift to patients as well. Great sense of humor! But very therapeutic interactions."

The Custom Service Ambassador at Summit said, "Robert would be a great chaplain at Alta Bates Summit Medical Center (ABSMC). He is very good with people, and I think that he would provide spiritual care at ABSMC...He is very diligent with his work." The staff chaplain wrote, "Great spirit, great energy. I have been getting excellent feedback from patients and staff about Robert's care. He is very diligent with his work. A great, reliable team member to have. Always ready to learn. Keep it up!"

In conclusion, my supervisor said, "You have blessed me and your peers with your devotion, courage, and authenticity. I especially appreciated your strong commitment to being a continuous learner, even with 30 years of ministry and professional functioning under your belt! Your courageous choice to be transparent and deeply trusting in our supervisory relationship while still sustaining professional boundaries was moving to me. I applaud your growth."

The growth I experienced in four months was unexpected. Though I entered this process with great apprehension, I felt grateful to have sustained the challenge. I was so elated to complete this unit that I invited my sisters, mother, and wife to participate in the graduation celebration. I wore a tuxedo because I felt as though I had won the lottery. Completing this second unit was a bridge to achieving my goal of being a Veteran Affairs (VA) chaplain. After completing this unit, I was able to apply to VA jobs in the area. I looked for employment within a sixty-mile radius, where I wouldn't have to drive or stay overnight.

While looking for a part-time job, I continued to substitute teach. Substitute teaching was my small way of giving back to society. I knew most of the middle schools and high schools didn't have African American males as teachers. My background gave the students a different perspective on life. I was not afraid to let students know I was an ordained minister with graduate degrees, 20 years of work in prison, and 20 years in the military. With this introduction, I challenged the myths young people had about image, low self-esteem, peer pressure, education, and their future. Whether it was in English or mathematics, I tried to make their education practical and relevant. In English classes, I encouraged students to keep a journal of their rhymes. If they were diligent, it would be easier to impress their friends and develop their own style and creativity.

As I continued to look for a VA job, I saw an opportunity in Reno, Nevada. I gathered my questions and went to the Travis Air Force Base Employment office and met with the Associate Directors for a mock interview. They obliged and drilled me on the potential questions. When the phone interview for Reno occurred, I felt I was ready. Two weeks after the interview in November, I was told by Chaplain Ed Tanner that I had passed the interview process. My reporting date was January 13th, 2013.

In November 2012, my wife and I made a major decision. One day, Susan came home very tired, and I asked, "Why are you working? You have thirty-five years on the books; why don't you retire?"

Relieved, Susan said, "Yeah, That's a great idea, when do we start?"

I said, "We can start looking for homes tomorrow!" This change would be a prime opportunity to use my VA loan. So, for the next few months, we looked at 37 different homes. We were glad our realtors, Tina and Tim, were working hard for us. In October 2012, I met Tina at a Reservist Fair at the Naval and Marine Corps Reserve Center. For years, I had been looking for a real estate person who was sincere about helping military servicemen use their VA loans. Tina appeared to be serious. After we made the decision, the process was intense as she made sure our home met all of the specifications.

Finally, we found out our present home had an open house only on Saturday and Sunday from 2 to 4 p.m. As soon as I walked upstairs to the game room, I sat on the floor and said to my wife, "This is it. I am tired of looking. This is it." Though I had to put $50,000 down to secure the home, I felt this was worth it. This home had everything we wanted: a 3-car garage, a backyard, plenty of space, spiral steps, and large walk-in closets. I was glad we had found at least one of our dream homes.

We had paid our dues, and I was looking forward to my wife quitting the workforce. Though it took time to get things together in Fairfield, we were able to move to our new Sacramento home in the first week of January. It was my job to get the van and make the move, but I enjoyed the process immensely.

After moving, the major issue was talking to the County Assessor and ensuring he did not add the $50,000 to the asking price. I made an appointment with him and explained my concern. I was grateful that he understood and was willing to ensure a fair process.

After the move, I prepared to go to Reno on Sunday and stayed at the Sands Hotel, which became my favorite hotel to stay at for my permanent intermittent job. The Sands was only fifteen minutes from work, and I always had a place to eat downstairs and a place to relax in the gym and jacuzzi.

It was a joy to meet Ed Tanner and his wife, who also worked at VA Sierra Hospital in Reno. Chaplain Tanner was a former Navy Chaplain, which meant we shared Navy stories in our spare time, but there was little spare time to talk about the Navy because VA Sierra was a 124-bed facility. Chaplain Tanner was very gracious about giving me free rein to sit in on the Mental Health Unit Interdisciplinary Meeting, the Palliative Care Meetings, and the Ethical Committees. With every meeting, I became more adept at communicating with the key players on each committee. Each committee enhanced my professional skills in new ways.

Chapter Thirty-Eight

Clean-Shaven

"Who do men say that I am?"
Mark 8:27

The beginning of 2013 brought a new sense of African-American pride to all of us. I reveled in the afterglow of President Obama's second inauguration. I was in the military; he was my commander-in-chief as well as our president. That impact lingered for a couple of days. Instead of celebrating Black History for one month, I thought, why don't we acknowledge it every day of the year? I tried to get the term "Black History 365" incorporated but had problems. I haven't given up yet. During the month of February and throughout the year, I posted popup profiles of famous African Americans on social media.

That January, I mentioned to my wife that this would be the year I would shave my head for two reasons. First, I was tired of trying to keep my wild hair laid down with a do-rag. Second, it was time to join the clean-look world. I'd had an abundance of hair all my life. In high school, I won recognition as the "best Afro." But it was time for another historic change. While my wife was away seeing her mom, I went to see my barber, Bela, at the McClellan Exchange.

I said, "Bela, shave it all off."

She said, "Okay."

Immediately following the shave, I went to the Exchange and bought a Norelco shaver. I walked outside, took a selfie of my shiny head, and texted it to my wife. She replied, "It looks good." I was freed. I was delivered from tied do-rags, pomades, combs, brushes, and all other hair paraphernalia. Hair care was easy. I just kept my shaver clean and washed my scalp. My mother didn't like my clean head, but she learned to live with it. Eventually, she gave up hope that I would grow it back. This liberating feeling gave me a new kind of connection made with Dad, who was bald at the end of his life because of chemo. Working on the oncology floor at the hospital, I was aware of the extra measure of rapport it gave me with chemo patients.

My shaved head gave me increased credibility with Marine Corps personnel who love "bald heads." Shortly after shaving my head, I started at Spokane, Washington, as the Commanding Officer of the Chaplains and Religious Program Specialists. I traveled there once a month. We had religious services during monthly drill weekends, where attendees shared their favorite songs on guitars. I recognized this was an anointed Reserve Center, though I found myself in some political tension with those under my command. I had noticed in Dallas, my previous assignment, and afterward in Spokane that faith was an important part of these communities. We averaged fifteen to twenty at services in every drill weekend for the two years I was stationed there.

What made this Reserve Center enticing was that the Spokane Veterans Affairs Hospital was next door. I was tempted to apply for the vacant VA permanent position there, but I knew my wife would not leave her friends in Sacramento. Still, the thought of fulfilling my dream as a VA chaplain stayed with me during my tenure there. Every week, I applied to programs that offered two units of CPE. Though I had two, I needed two more to qualify for a permanent position. Finally, after searching for eighteen months, a two-unit CPE program opened at Sutter

Roseville Medical Center for the fiscal year 2013-14. I was elated. All things had worked together for good. Buying the home in Sacramento, getting the job in Reno, and now the final piece of getting these last two units of CPE made me feel God had orchestrated the desires of my heart.

The crowning blessing of my military career was being assigned as the Deputy Force Chaplain at Pacific Forces, Camp Smith, Hawaii. I had served there before, so I was familiar with the protocol. Oahu, Hawaii, was my first Annual Training site in 1994, and this assignment capped my career on the island where I had started. The challenge was finding air transportation to get there every two months. Fortunately, I knew Dottie Williams, who ensured I got a reserved seat on MAC flights— Military Airlift Command that transported active-duty personnel subject to available space. I was blessed to have a vehicle I could leave at Travis Air Force Base while I rode in a C-5 to Hickam Air Force Base. My housing was always comfortable, and my luggage was never out of my presence. This assignment allowed me to exercise and go on special hikes and excursions on the weekends.

During that same time, right before I started my two units of CPE at Roseville, my supervisor, Chaplain Tanner, left VA Sierra Nevada to take a supervisory job at VA Asheville, North Carolina. Since his extended family was on the East Coast, this was a strategic move for him. His departure allowed me to accrue more hours at VA Sierra Nevada. I spent my time between Reno, Nevada, and Sutter Roseville. This was a busy time of work, education, group sharing, and supervisory training. I was excited to be surrounded by a gender-balanced group of colleagues—two women and three men. There was nothing unusual about this group, except my supervisor was a Latter Day Saint (LDS), as was one of my colleagues. Supervisory time gave me the opportunity to talk through questions I'd had for a long time about the LDS faith. I wondered why the LDS community from 1849 to 1978 prevented men of African descent from being ordained to the priesthood. Since 1978, I have loved to discuss this issue with LDS individuals I met and listened to their biblical reasons for the prohibition. It was comical to hear the justifications that had no biblical legitimacy, but I tried to listen with honest curiosity and understanding. I heard and saw personal testimony from my supervisor and classmates. Basically, they confessed that the prohibition of African men was a decision by the hierarchy of the church. However, both my supervisor and colleague did not feel this was a position shared by most of the LDS members. They were glad that the prohibition had been lifted. Though I accepted their accounts of how they came to terms with this doctrine, I wanted to know how these individuals felt being raised with this explicit racial discrimination in the polity of their faith. Though we talked about vulnerability, this was an area they did not want to explore. I will continue to dialogue about this issue as long as there is one LDS individual willing to have the conversation. I believe the sect carries secrets and fosters covert feelings of racism that need to be addressed.

Though I did not invite my entire family to the graduation in May 2014, I was ecstatic to be completing my final two units. This five-year process began in July 2009. Following this CPE path from the first to the fourth unit was a journey on which I had had few cheerleaders. This path was encouraged, but only by one person I knew in the Navy who had followed the CPE and VA route as a career. I hoped I was paving new ground for someone else.

I was rewarded for my diligence: shortly following the completion of the fourth unit, I was hired full-time at VA Sierra Nevada. The final step of the CPE process was getting board-certified. I applied to the National Association of Veteran Affairs Chaplain (NAVAC) for certification. They sent me a letter indicating that the Presenter of the Certification Committee would be Juliana Lesher, with two panel members. They would be my oral examiners. Juliana Lesher was the Chief Chaplain of the San Antonio VA and was well-respected in the VA Chaplain ranks. From June to the interview date, October 28th, I studied. The interview process was based on twenty-four professional Chaplain Competencies. I unearthed every note, theory, and didactic that had helped me over the past five years.

I was challenged to visit patients in those months, realizing my whole future came down to passing this Certification Exam. I knew I would see the Committee members at a meeting in the future, so I wanted to make a good impression. The Presenter summarized my life for the committee: "Father-ordained Methodist elder who served as a pastor until his death; Grandparents and parents were all very devout in this faith; Raised in the Christian Methodist Episcopal Church with several hiatuses from the CME church; Disability of stuttering was a challenge to overcome. Conquering the speech hurdle gave him the confidence to conquer other hurdles, the ability to write, and the ability to write well with the skill of the prophets." Lesher mentioned that at the age of six, I felt the urge to serve God in ministry. The letter from the staff through five years of CPE indicated I was a man dedicated to God and committed to his family, who knows boundaries and practices good self-care. I received a doctorate level and served in prisons as a US Navy Chaplain, and I currently serve in Reno and Mather VA Centers. The stage was set. My whole life had prepared me for such a time as this.

Chapter Thirty-Nine

Living the Dream

"Beloved now are we the children of God, and it has not yet been revealed what we shall be, but we know that when He is revealed, we shall be like Him, for we shall see Him as He is."
1 John 3:2

On the morning of Tuesday, October 28th, 2014, I woke up early and prayed for an hour. I needed every favor and mercy available to calm my heart and direct my mind for this auspicious day. I left for work in my three-piece suit, prepared to impress the Certification Committee with words and wisdom. I looked over my Performance Appraisal and highlighted where I felt Exceptional and Fully Successful. I was glad the President of the panel, Juliana Lesher, was open to starting promptly and directly and gave me a mock interview to ensure everything was in order. The official interview lasted one hour, and all three individuals appeared satisfied with my responses. Within a few days, I received results that showed that I had passed my Certification Panel. When I heard the news, I called my wife and couldn't wait to go out and celebrate. I thanked God, lifting my hands. I gave a shout to the Lord for bringing me this far by faith.

Just when I thought my life would get easier, the job situation became worse. I began noticing that my supervisor was saying or implying negative racial slurs in front of me and behind my back. I documented the incidents of implicit bias and sent a copy to the Affirmative Action Officer. I was on guard, especially when I ventured up to the executive floor, where the supervisor's office was situated next to the Director's. Fortunately, the Director had an open-door policy. I was glad she understood my dilemma. During our discussion, she explained the difficulty of handling employee complaints about high-level executives. Despite the complexity of her own decision, I felt exonerated that my Report of Action was supported by the Director.

Next, I applied for the Chief of Chaplains position at our facility. Unfortunately, they chose a chaplain from Charleston, South Carolina. On the first day of his supervision, the phone rang three times, and he didn't pick it up. Afterward, I realized this chaplain not only had a hearing problem but his vision was also impaired. Everything he read had to be enlarged to 24-point font. I tried to show compassion, but I had expected someone who could, at least, hear and see. His leadership was also demoralizing. He claimed that he was the first chaplain to start every program that had ever existed in the VA. Humility was not his strong suit. After three months, the same Associate Director that I was having implicit bias issues with, told him that his rogue behavior was unacceptable. The following week, I came to work and found he had left because he had received a vote of "No Confidence."

After he left, I was promoted to Chief of Chaplains for the VA Sierra Nevada Health Care System. This advancement was the pinnacle of a long journey. The feedback, critique, and constant searching for one unit here and two units there for five years was worth the effort. Driving two hours from Sacramento to Reno for four years through hail, windstorms, and snow was my resilience training. Yes, I had paid my dues and watched individuals who were less qualified come and try to discredit me. As Chief, I was given the opportunity to hire, train, and guide chaplains as needed. It was a joy to employ individuals who could lighten my counseling load so I didn't have to be constantly on-call. I took my job seriously and moved to Reno to be available daily. This was a costly decision for both my wife and me. She understood, but it was a challenging time for us. I continued to report discrimination issues as they occurred.

The bittersweet memory of 2015 was bringing my Navy career to a close. I planned to have my retirement ceremony during the December drill because my middle daughter Naivasha was able to come from New York, and I wanted her and my youngest daughter, Kayla, to be present. Although the retirement was moved to January 2016, both daughters were able to attend my annual birthday party in December. My family of origin was glad to have at least two of my children at the annual event. Getting together with family has been challenging since my divorce from Angel. Everybody wanted to take a picture with these two daughters because we didn't know when we would all be together again.

During the January ceremony, I appreciated seeing my CPE friends, supervisor, and Navy and Marine Corps friends I served with over the years. The ceremony was at the Sacramento Reserve Center and was performed decently and in order. I enjoyed giving flowers to my wife and Kayla. The Honor Guard ritually unfolded, folded, and presented a flag that had been flown at my last duty station, PAC Forces, Camp Smith, HI, as they played "Old Glory."

When I returned to Reno, I settled into the challenging task of pastoral care at a busy 124-bed hospital, twice the capacity of the Northern CA Health Care System in Sacramento. I balanced the tasks of listening and supervising while hiking during the week and on weekends. During 2015, I felt I had received "the Spirit of John Muir." Muir, a mechanical genius and trained botanist, took immense delight in the natural beauty he found in the wild. He would sit for hours on a granite overlook, sketching or journaling, until he became raptured in communion with the "divine wildness" of the Sierra landscapes. My spirit had an insatiable desire to explore the hills and mountains of Yosemite and every place Muir had ventured. I had started going to Yosemite in 1968, where Dad preached every available fifth Sunday at Glacier Point.

The acknowledgment of Muir's spirit led to an epiphany that I needed to climb Half Dome. Hiking became my passion. All I needed were my hiking sticks, camera, hat, gloves, and an iPhone to capture all the memories. I used these photos and journals in my meditation group with mental health patients and later in the 12-step programs I facilitated. Every morning, I prayed and walked outside to view the incredible sunrise in the sky. I felt God was sending messages with red, yellow, and orange rays from the seventh heaven. When I saw this, I knew all things were possible.

Right before the Lenten season that year, I got the opportunity to visit Hampton, VA, and participate in Chaplain Training. I had waited since 2013 to go to this training, so when it happened in 2016, it was another dream come true. What an honor to meet all the individuals I had heard on conference calls over the years. I got the opportunity to be in residence at the Chaplain School and see how everybody was trained. I invited my wife Susan to visit me the first weekend, and we stayed in spacious lodging at Langley. We enjoyed visiting Virginia Beach, a place Susan had enjoyed during her youth and young adulthood. I was immensely excited to dine with the mentors of the school and gain credibility with these mighty men and women of God.

During Lent, I had another epiphany about wanting to carry a cross. One of my friends in Fairfield, CA, had a church, and he planned to walk through Fairfield to the Courthouse carrying the cross on Good Friday. I came down that Friday and joined

Pastor Hill in this symbolic journey. What an awesome reflection to think about what Jesus had to endure on his walk to Golgotha's hill. Though the cross that Pastor Hill created was only 25 pounds, this endeavor gave us an inkling of what Jesus experienced. Adventures with Pastor Hill always drew me closer to the cross. It was an enduring focus of his own devotions and preaching.

A month earlier, I had the novel thought of writing my memoir. Because I had reached the pinnacle of my CPE career as Chief, I felt it was a good time to chronicle the turning points that led to this mountaintop experience. Though the memoir group that I joined was great on the technical side, I felt they seemed to dismiss the significance of the spiritual part of my journey. The memoir leadership tried everything possible not to offend any person of faith. In the process, I could not testify to the power and encouragement that faith had given me over the years.

As chief in Reno, I was in the epicenter of God's will. Though I was cautious around my supervisor, with her recommendation, I got the opportunity to speak about Moral Injury to a large gathering of nurses at the National Association of Nurses, Reno. They liked the presentation so much that they invited me to speak again the following year. After this pastoral care offering in Reno, I couldn't wait to travel with my friends to fulfill the epiphany God gave me about climbing Half Dome. After speaking on Thursday, I packed up my hiking gear and headed out.

Chapter Forty

A Partaker of Grace

"The steps of a good man are ordered by the Lord: and He delights in his way. Though he falls, he shall not be utterly cast down: for the Lord upholds him with His hand."
Psalm 37: 23-24

For once, I want to tell the truth about the Half Dome Hike. In September 2015, while hiking in Yosemite National Park, I had an epiphany. This epiphany centered on climbing one of the rock formations in the park, Half Dome. The last time I had a similar epiphany in Kenya, in 1975, I felt prompted to climb Mt. Kilimanjaro, which I accomplished in 1976.

I shared this novel idea with my climbing comrade, Grey. I thought June 2016 would be a good time to attempt it. Grey is a professional hiker born in Carson City, having spent his entire life exploring the Sierras and the Pacific Crest Trail. It was humbling to hike with him and his dog, Cowboy, because he pushed my limits. Since I lived and worked in Reno during that year, Yosemite was a constant possibility.

For nine months, we took five-to-seven-mile hikes to get acclimated to the Half Dome challenge. I joined a couple of hiking groups for added experience. One group hiked on Mondays and Thursdays, and another on Saturdays. These experiences were the ultimate for learning about the trees, estimating water needs, and group fellowship.

During the practice hikes, I never lost track of my epiphanal goal. We reserved lodging three months ahead of time and placed our bid in the lottery to ascend Half Dome. We asked a friend, Frank, to accompany us. We left on the fourth Friday in June and traveled in Grey's car. When we got to the campsite, the beds in the tents were spaciously arranged. We were glad the dining room and showers were close by. We checked our backpacks to see if we had enough water and snacks to last the entire 14.2-mile trek.

Saturday morning, we headed to the parking area before getting on the trail leading to Vernal Falls. On the path, I lost my sunglasses at the first scenic view. My eyes were sensitive, so I hoped a headache would not develop along the path. I wore my hiking backpack filled with two liters of water and planned to fill up at the first stop. I was glad I brought hiking sticks for balance. I was equipped for this feat.

After reaching the bridge to fill our CamelBaks, we took the easier path to the falls. This path seemed effortless in comparison to the alternate mist trail route. When we arrived at the next major stop, Nevada Falls, we took a break to check our supplies two-thirds of the way up the mountain. The rest was about pace.

During the last third of the journey, we started noticing springs along the path. Though we had completed our paperwork, we were not selected for the lottery of the day. Praying for a favor, we asked the female Ranger, who said, "No permit, no climb." I didn't feel bad about the decision because we hadn't brought enough water; we'd already drunk more than we'd anticipated. As we took pictures, Frank and I suddenly realized we couldn't locate Grey. We looked everywhere without success.

Finally, we decided to make the descent without him. We got to Nevada Falls without difficulty, but the sun was bearing down, and water consumption was still a problem. As we looked at the springs going down the hill, we wanted to fill our

CamelBak's with water, but Grey had the water-purifying tablets. So, we slowed down our pace and took the shorter route. I noticed Frank had problems navigating the rocks, so I gave him one of my hiking poles. He maneuvered better with at least one pole. When we got to Vernal Falls, we took another break. We knew the next stage might be challenging because the mist trail was drenched, and the dry path was slippery. I took my time coming down the dry steps from Vernal Falls. I walked more slowly because I only had one hiking pole. As I stepped down from the last stone step onto the sand, something happened. The next conscious moment, somebody told me, "Stay where you are, don't go anywhere." I looked down, and I saw blood had stained the rock at my feet.

A person kept asking me questions. I wondered what had happened. Somebody told me that after the last step, I had fallen and slid at least thirty feet. The only thing that stopped my downward slide was this bloodied raised rock. The incident was a blur. I have no memory of it. Six members of the Rescue Team showed up.

They asked a series of critical care questions, "Do you have any broken bones?" I didn't know. "Do you want to be airlifted to Fresno or driven to the local hospital in Mariposa?" Grey had just reappeared amid the emergency because he almost succumbed to a heat stroke. I thought about the cost and my friend's situation and decided, "Take me to the local hospital." They put my neck in a brace, placed me on a six-foot board, and guided the Big Wheel four thousand steps to the bottom of the valley. To reduce expenses, we decided to use Grey's car instead of the ambulance.

At the Mariposa Hospital, I got a CT scan. There were no broken bones. I was just scratched and bruised, with deep marks on my left scalp and face. I was glad my sunglasses were lost because plastic pieces could have pierced my eye. After the sunset, it was too dark to return to base camp, so we stayed at

the home of one of Grey's friends in Mariposa. We asked Grey
about his disappearance, and he explained he had a heat stroke
attack, which forced him to get water quickly. It was helpful to
know because we had been very anxious about his disappearance. The next day, with a new pair of sunglasses and an un-
shaven face, I went with the two of them to pick up our belongings. We walked along Tioga Lake. I looked like Scarface, but
I was glad to be alive. This ordeal made me thankful for supportive friends.

When I returned to Reno, I tried to understand the lessons
from this experience. The desire to climb Half Dome was
strong, though I did not anticipate the trauma of the fall or
Grey's sudden absence due to overheating. I thought Frank
would have been prepared by bringing his own hiking sticks. I
believe if I had not lent him my other hiking stick, the falling
accident would not have happened. A lot of would-have, could-
have, should-have scenarios entered my mind at the time, but I
pressed on.

Still, I was alive and grateful the facial scars were not permanent. I looked like an ugly duckling, but my mind was stable.
I could easily have slipped into the waterfall if the rock had not
stopped my slide. I was happy; I had the presence of mind to
choose an escort on foot by the Rescue Team: the expenses for
the evacuation came to over $50,000, but the VA and Kaiser
health plans covered my expenses. It took over a year to resolve
the bill, but I was grateful for excellent health care.

During the summer of 2016, I received an offer to work at
the Northern California Health Care System in Sacramento.
The supervisor at Sacramento VA promised a salary increase,
but it never materialized. I felt it was time to get back to the
home front. For four years, I had spent Sunday afternoons driving to Reno and Friday evenings trying to get back home. During the winter, this two-hour trek turned into four-hour drudg-
ery behind snowplows and sixteen-wheelers. As I prepared to

move back to Sacramento, I got a chance to resolve the racial issue with my supervisor. A few weeks before leaving, I turned in my final Report of the Incident. Afterward, the supervisor, who was an Associate Director, came under increased scrutiny. Changes were made, and I felt satisfied with the way I handled the racial discrimination charges for eighteen months. I counseled fellow employees never to go home stressed when there was undue supervisory pressure. Everybody had a recourse, which involved reporting the problems. Being able to give that advice to others made my counseling time with other VA staff more effective.

Susan continued to take care of her mother, Bessie, in Virginia, and I struggled with my new job responsibilities. It was a challenge adjusting to being a chaplain without being in charge. Statistics that came out at the end of the fiscal year revealed I was performing 60% of the pastoral care in the hospital, with two other higher-paid chaplains on board. No one evaluating me took that into consideration, but I was never able to voice my concerns about the work disparity. One has to use wisdom about when to complain because it may adversely affect the Fiscal Performance Appraisal.

For self-care, I took respite at the ocean or Muir Woods. Marin County restored my soul with solitude and a grateful history. Just remembering how far I had come from those years of seminary gave me perspective. Reflecting on the past empowered me to press on despite difficulties.

With Susan consumed with elder care, I continued to see my family of origin and my nearest daughter, Kayla, in Oakland. I was glad Kayla was still nearby. With Alecia in the Dallas area and Naivasha between Los Angeles and New York, it was good to maintain a local father-daughter connection. Susan's absence gave me an opportunity to visit with others who had been supportive over the years.

At Sacramento VA, one department appreciated my care and professional expertise. I found the Behavioral Health Intensive Care Unit (BHICU) was particularly supportive of my time with the patients. One reason I could relate to the BHICU patients was because I was the only clinician who had served in the military. The patients knew I cared about their plight, as I spoke every week in group and shared on Sunday mornings. I tried weekly to help each one with the transition from being a soldier to being a civilian. There is a transitional period from being told what to do to making decisions on your own. Often, the challenge of suddenly making a range of adult decisions causes suicidal ideation.

The Christmas party with the BHICU staff was a game-changer for me. The trainee psychologists and psychiatrists looked at my progress notes and noticed the connection I had with the patients. The party gave me the opportunity to meet with the team in a casual setting. Having rapport with the clinicians helped me listen to them in a new way. An effective Interdisciplinary Team lets the patient know that teamwork is therapeutic. I felt I was the transitional team member who made the difference for the service-connected VA patient.

After that event, all the clinicians made me part of their orientation for their students. When student nurses entered the unit, I gave them an orientation by letting them sit in my class on repairing moral injury and asking questions. After Sunday services, the clinicians asked me to do a Chaplain Assessment to be included in the progress notes. They saw that chaplains looked at more than the physical, social, moral, and emotional history. The clinicians saw that our pastoral care training was not only sophisticated but also often revealed an aspect of the patient that was not part of what they were trained to consider.

I loved having one-on-one counseling sessions to assess what other clinicians did not see. I loved the collaboration and trust that developed over time. My four quadrants of well-being included body, mind, community, and spirituality. These quadrants were used as instructional pillars in the military and worked perfectly as pillars for patients going through transitions. I believe my presence in the BHICU environment made a difference.

Chapter Forty-One

Surviving Stormy Weather

"Precious in the sight of the LORD is the death of His saints."
Psalm 116:15

Susan's mother, Bessie Wade, passed away during the first week of December 2016. She was the most gracious mother-in-law of my three marriages. We talked, prayed, and sang to each other with ease. In her later years, Bessie experienced symptoms of dementia and Alzheimer's disease. Amid physical and mental health issues, Bessie's faith in Jesus remained strong. Susan told me Bessie would often sit outside and call out, "Jesus, Jesus." She anticipated Jesus' presence as if she were waiting for her children to return from school.

I totally approved of Susan's retirement desire to spend time with her mother. It was challenging for her sister, Judie, in Virginia to meet all their mother's needs. With both sisters available, they took turns visiting the Skilled Nursing Facility to consult with the nursing staff. Living twenty-six hundred miles from home, Susan constantly expressed her desire to see her family of origin. I never asked her to come home during her caregiving there unless she needed a break.

When I traveled east for the funeral, I met cousins and relatives Susan had mentioned during our 16 years of marriage for the first time. This was not a mournful occasion but a Homegoing. In the African-American Christian funeral tradition, the homegoing celebrates a person's return to their heavenly home. Bessie raised three children: Jerry Wade, Judie Pierce, and Susan. Mother Wade had taken them to church and still, at the end of her life, played her tambourine. She was small in stature but mighty in the spirit. After the funeral, Susan stayed a few weeks to resolve probate issues with her sister.

Susan returned three days before Christmas to enjoy our family gathering at my younger sister Kelesha's home in Stockton. The family enjoyed seeing Susan and gave her encouraging words of condolence. We celebrated our anniversary at Yoshi's, a Japanese restaurant and jazz club, with my sisters and their husbands. We were entertained by an old-school singing group called Bloodstone.

In January 2017, a colleague and I started a 12-step program at the Sacramento VA. As veterans, both Rosie, a devout social worker, and I felt experienced enough to help struggling veterans through their daily struggles with addiction. The Chapel department purchased unique 12-step Bibles, so we followed the commentary for each step. This group was the ideal group to discuss how the truths of the Bible helped with effective living.

After eight years of historic leadership by President Obama, I felt a spirit of doom descend at the election of Donald Trump. The African-American community was so traumatized we just called the Commander-in-Chief "45." After eight years of impressive executive guidance, 45 was more than a letdown. To encourage the community, I wrote a poem entitled "Now We Heal."

Now we start the process, now we start the decree,
From a place of agony to a place of walking free;
This walk will impact the essence of our inside,
Our heart, even the tears we have cried;

We'll learn resilience of fighting in the pit,

Dispelling darts and arrows, dealing with hypocrites;
Through it all, we'll become focused and succinct,
Find ways to connect our causes and truly link;

I believe in the human spirit, especially in defeat,
The ability to rise from ashes in the midst of the heat;
Grieve if you must take a nap from all the stress,
Then, wake up determined and ready to address;

Tell the truth by your actions, be genuine in your speech,
Teach your children, and be available to preach;
We'll survive, my friends, if we walk together,
We've proved we can handle any weather!

A day after the inauguration, a million women marched for women's rights to protest the presidency of 45. My wife and I joined thousands who marched in the rain at the state capitol. We felt "we the people" had to do something positive to manage our frustration.

As a proactive move, in February 2017, I took a trip to Costa Rica to discuss community organization from a spiritual perspective. I traveled with Yvette, the good friend I had dated in college. I trekked to this country to be supportive of Yvette's endeavors, but I think she expected more from our travels together. This trip was a timely excursion to talk about ways to be more effective in our community. I appreciate the invitation. Being in a rainforest, like the Amazon, reminded me of my time in the Peace Corps. Though I knew very little Spanish, I spent a few months on Duolingo and learned some basic salutations. My Spanish tutorials were timely because, on arrival, I spent the first day on an unexpected excursion. I immediately got a guide who took me to a volcano and a game park. I spent an hour at the volcano and three at the park, taking pictures of waterfalls, toucans, butterflies, leaping frogs, poisonous frogs, and other amphibious creatures.

After the tour, I joined members of our group to head to our destination for the week, Puriscal. The location was two hours from San Jose, in a place where agriculture was emphasized. I loved the agricultural fields but didn't like the constant noise of cicadas at night. My acute hearing could also detect jaguars growling. We slept in an open bed with mosquito netting. I felt as though I was back in Kenya, fighting off the same malaria-carrying Anopheles mosquitoes.

We discussed practicums on how to maintain spiritual health amid power politics. For a week, we learned how to harness our organizational strength. In between classes, we took hikes, learned how to use the land effectively, and cooked meals to enhance community building. Living in Puriscal was an educational experience. I learned that 50 percent of Costa Rica was made up of primary rainforest, and 28 percent of the oxygen produced on earth comes from the rainforest. I was glad Yvette had invited me because this trip gave me first-hand knowledge of the detrimental effects of deforestation and global warming.

Two weeks after returning home, we were invited by Dr. Winsome Jackson and her husband, Dr. Rudy Pearson, to a "Discussion with Colson Whitehead." Whitehead received the Pulitzer Prize for *The Underground Railroad* and later *The Nickel Boys*. This was another opportunity to meet a literary giant. Twenty years before, I had met Maya Angelou, who spoke at our prison and invited a small group to her home. Within the past ten years, I had sat behind Alice Walker several times at church and interviewed Gil Scott-Heron, the jazz poet, singer, and author. Colson was one of several extremely creative artists who had graced my life. I was humbled to be in the presence of creative genius, and I felt they blessed my journey.

Later, in the month of March, I flew to Los Angeles to listen to my middle daughter Naivasha's life. I slept at her place and listened to her world. As we walked to the Convention Center, I noticed her interchanges with athletic friends who were there for a conference. We took pictures as she walked around in fashionable athletic garb. We went to a health food restaurant Vasha frequented and met one of her male friends who worked there. I also got the opportunity to go to a speakeasy where Naivasha was facilitating a conversation about community issues. During the visit, Vasha shared some of the frustration she felt that I had missed so much of her life. I'd had no idea about most of the things she expressed. I didn't know she'd been in eight marathons. There was no way I would have known unless Naivasha or her mother, Angel, had told me. Naivasha and I had challenges from time to time communicating by phone or text. I wish the communication could have been better. I continue to love her and send love weekly, realizing sometimes That's all we can do for our children.

The end of the summer brought one of the happiest moments experienced in my life. A high school friend, Bobby Clements, asked me to officiate at the wedding of his daughter, Danielle. Almost ten years earlier, in 2006, Bobby had asked me to officiate at the funeral service for his mother, Hafeezah. I prayed with her for one week before eulogizing her. Now, eleven years later, I feel privileged to assist the family in another important ritual. I counseled the couple for a few sessions and emailed a template of the marital vows. The ceremony was scheduled for Pismo Beach, California, in the picturesque days of October. Bobby purchased our room and made our time enjoyable for the wedding rehearsal and the dinner afterward. I basked in meeting Bobby's extended family from Switzerland, other parts of Europe, and all over the United States. Bobby was divorced, but he has traveled extensively.

On the day of the wedding, Bobby was proud to escort his daughter down the aisle to the bridal arch positioned forty feet from the edge of the cliff. As I administered these marital vows,

I was humbled to be part of this celebration. It was a wedding fit for a princess and the kind I would love for any of my daughters.

I have realized that it was not a coincidence that I have stayed in contact with Bobby. I wondered during high school how a guy of his modest stature played football without injury. I was informed he played Pop Warner as a youth and learned all the building blocks of football. How I wished I'd had that training. Interestingly, Bobby was fascinated by how people gravitated toward me. In our later years, we have shared an appreciation for life, relationships, and the situations that continue to teach us about resilience, community, and authentic friendship.

Chapter Forty-Two

Black Panthers

*"A man who has friends must himself be friendly, but there is
a friend who sticks closer than a brother."*
Proverbs 18:24

November brought the presentation of my sister's one-person play, *Forgivable*. Ronita wrote a book in 2012 called *Coming to Forgiveness*. Now, five years later, she had adapted the thoughts and feelings from that book into a three-act performance. I was extremely proud of Ro's ability to enter new creative territory. This need to prove oneself was a family theme. Each of my siblings was driven to use their skills to the optimum. Part of our drive stemmed from our inability to attend the college of our dreams.

In 1965, Ro told my parents, "I would love to attend Howard University and be around people of color."

Our parents responded, "That's too far."

"But we have relatives in Washington, D.C., for family support."

"We don't have the money. We just bought this new house."

I faced the same resistance six years later when I wanted to go to Morehouse. I thought this would be an easy decision because Dad had worked with Dr. Martin Luther King, Jr., Morehouse's most famous alum, for three years. But my parents denied my request and said they didn't think I was mature enough to go to school in Atlanta.

These denials could have caused long-term trauma, but later in life, we found ways to compensate for these disappointments. Ronita's one-person play was another way of recouping her dreams, and in the process, she became another role model of manifestation. She motivated me to show up and perform to the best of my ability. During my three Bay Area pastorates, Ronita supported me with her world-class musicianship at the piano and strategic leadership. When my plate became a platter, she counseled me through difficult times in ministry. Our love and appreciation for each other have continued to grow.

2017 ended with birthday celebrations, anniversary festivities, and new beginnings. One consistent theme for our family is the need to experience those once-in-a-lifetime adventures. As January rolled around, many of the family prepared for the Soul Train cruise. Ronita and John talked about the 2107 cruise with such excitement that the other family members were ecstatic to join them on the 2018 version. I had been on thirty cruises since 1975, but never on an adventure where music filled the stairways, elevators, dining hall, and every space where people gathered. Having served as a disc jockey for four years and a member of two bands, I was familiar with the tunes of the seventies. Not only was the music stirring, but we got a chance to meet the musicians as they roamed throughout the ship.

A highlight was seeing Jeffrey Osborne leave the stage and walk up the stairs to serenade us from the balcony. At the after-parties, we shook hands with members of The Whispers. The entire cruise was an exceptional experience. Every day, musicians we had listened to and loved for years were standing next to us in the food line.

It was edifying to be surrounded by African-American people loving our culture and music. I was even able to meet an

African-American Marine Corps general as part of the Military Appreciation. I had served with several admirals and generals My first assignment was to give devotionals to three and four-star generals, but rarely did I get an opportunity to have a private audience with a general. With our group of eight, we were able to save seats to ensure we received the best seats for each cruise activity.

One bonus of this trip was meeting an earthly angel named Sabrina. Through the years, I've noticed on Facebook Sabrina has befriended several musicians and comedians. She has the gift of encouragement and affirmation and is a cheerleader for anyone who steps on stage. The added blessing of meeting her is that she lives in the Bay Area, which has allowed us to encourage one another through social media and in person.

The Soul Cruise theme of Love, Peace, and Soul continued to reverberate in our lives as we returned home for the movie premiere of *Black Panther*. Since college, my spirit has yearned to find powerful, sustaining stories about the continent and the resilient cultures of Africa. Two and a half years of living in Kenya merely scratched the surface of my explorations. I had wanted to receive this history at a Historical Black College or University (HBCU). From age nine, I had always thought I was destined to attend an HBCU. My father took me to football games at Grambling State University, where he was an instructor. Mom attended Southern University A & M, so I thought attending an HBCU was a foregone conclusion. When we moved west to California, matriculating at an HBCU became a long-shot dream.

At every opportunity, I took advantage of every educational opportunity. Historically, Hollywood had done a terrible job of accurately representing members of minority groups. When they were portrayed, they were often seen as intellectually inferior and sexually aggressive towards white women. The premiere of

Black Panther in 2018 created positive archetypes rarely seen on the screen.

For the first time, my wife and I dressed up in African garb before viewing a movie. I was dressed in a gold four-piece Agbada with black Kofi and Susan, a black top, and a head-piece. Throughout the two-hour movie, I felt African pride. I understood the Swahili words and knew first-hand the brilliance of Africans from the classroom. I was ecstatic speaking about the movie on social media and at work.

To extend my discussion of Wakanda, I bought a ball cap with the words, "Make Wakanda Great Again." This was a parody of the Make America Great Again hat worn by Republicans at that point. I knew America was great because it was built on the blood, sweat, and tears of African-Americans. Very few individuals acknowledged this fact, so I created my own way to educate the populace.

This involvement in African-American education continued when the Sacramento VA found money to send me to a conference in March 2018. I was finally able to attend the Black Chaplain Conference in San Diego, which I had been wanting to attend since 2013. I was thrilled because I was so familiar with the host city. It was a joy to network and meet the executive staff and the presenters. The information shared was an asset to my 12-step and mental health program groups. Being in San Diego allowed me to visit the Escondido Safari Park and Carlsbad Field of Flowers during personal time. The African-American networking enriched my professional experience.

In April, we flew to Washington, D.C. to be present for the Cherry Blossom Festival in the nation's capital. This vacation also allowed us to deepen our understanding of another part of our heritage. Six months prior, I had found out that my grandmother on my mother's side was Choctaw. That knowledge led us to explore the Native American Indian Museum and dig deeper into the story of the Trail of Tears. I was shocked to find that every treaty the U.S. government made with Indians from 1778 to 1871 was broken by the white man, 500 treaties in all. This was an American History they never taught us in school. This new information fueled my fire for further truth.

I found that truth in the National Museum of African American History & Culture, which we visited for three days straight. The design gave the visitor the sense they had been captured and put on slave ships. We got the chance to envision what it felt like to be chained, sleeping next to one another for long voyages. As we moved from floor to floor, I realized one thing I had never seen was the picture of my grandfather's birth certificate on my father's side. When I viewed it, I saw on the bottom in bold red letters, "Cannot Read or Write." I had never seen a birth certificate like this, and to know it was my kin put a new purpose in my spirit. Now, I understood why Dad was passionate about education. My grandfather was a presser and a tailor, so he eventually learned to read and write. His certificate came out of the Jim Crow South that didn't allow blacks to have educational privileges.

Every word I write is an indictment against the racist system that perpetuates illiteracy as one form of injustice. After going to the African American Museum, we ventured to Frederick Douglass' House and saw his mentors positioned on his wall. Douglas continues to be a driving force in my life for historical truth. His portrait hangs on my wall. One hundred and seventy-five years after his impact on abolitionist speeches, his words still ring true in my heart and in the soul of America.

Chapter Forty-Three

Redemption through Action

"Now, when these things begin to happen, look up and lift up your heads, because your redemption draws near."
Luke 21:28

After visiting the Native American National Museum in Washington, D.C., I received an invitation to pray at a VA training in Redding, California. Because of my recent visit to the museum and discovery of my Choctaw heritage, I handled this prayer invitation differently.

For the first time, I prayed, "I acknowledge the ancestors of Redding and the Wintu tribe. If it had not been for this tribe, Redding would have never been developed. I pray this VA meeting will maintain the sacredness of these grounds and never allow any mandate to destroy the spirit of brotherhood." After the meeting, members of the community responded positively to my mention of the Native American impact on the community. I am glad my eyes were finally opened to realize every settlement in America was on land once owned by Native Americans. The reality of this brutal truth brought tears and keeps me humble whenever I am tempted to lift American pride. I am glad that time and broadened public consciousness have helped heal the wounds caused by the spirit of the Wild West.

In my family, I finally got the opportunity for redemption. Over the course of my marriage with Susan, I often worked elsewhere when she had to go through medical procedures. When the time came for me to be available, there was often a scheduling conflict. I was glad I was informed this time so I could take time off to support her. It was humbling to transport Susan to the hospital, be present during pre-op, and be available during post-op. I was glad that I was aware of the whole surgery process. It calmed my anxiety to be there. I was also glad to be available for my wife and do what any loving husband wants to do for their spouse.

In another part of my family life, I got an opportunity to organize our annual father-daughter getaway. This year, our destination was Mendocino on the northern coast of California. Susan and I had spent several weekends here, and I had ventured there alone when Susan was away taking care of her mother. I was glad Kayla was available once again to accompany me to the coast.

On every trip we made together, Kayla appeared just as excited as I was to travel. I was blessed that she also enjoyed going to different places. Though I loved being near water, my former wife, Angel, had never allowed me to take my daughters to the ocean. Therefore, my daughters never got to experience one of my great loves. Fortunately, Kayla has shared some of my affinities because she lives within 100 miles of my residence. Whenever we have been in the same space, I pray we can grow closer. I hoped we could take time for conversation and create synergy. Our conversations resembled this type of normalcy:

"Kayla, how's it going?"

"Nothing new, same old thing."

"What does 'nothing new' mean? Same job?"

"Yes, same job, more responsibility, venturing out of the office more."

"Are you satisfied with what you do?"

" Well, I am getting a little tired of my fellow employees just doing the normal without really caring about their job."

"How so?"

"You know, part of my job is keeping restaurants in compliance with food and cleanliness standards. Well, some of my fellow workers are more concerned about passing the inspection than really looking closer at what's going on."

I appreciated Kayla's conscientiousness and her care for real quality service.

Inquiring about her social life, I asked, "How's your concert volunteering?"

Kayla said, "I have seen some interesting comedians at the Fox Theater lately. They gave me a few laughs."

"That's great; I'm glad you keep up with what's happening in the millennial generation. And how's your exercise program? Are you still doing trapeze on Tuesday?"

"Yes, but I only go twice a month, where I used to go every week."

"I would love to go with you one time. All that sounds exciting."

That was usually the gist of our conversation. One of the reasons I liked traveling with Kayla was that the travel expanded our conversational horizon. We usually left early Friday morning, and I asked if Kayla would be able to spend the night on Thursday so we could get an early start. She slept most of the way up to Mendocino because it had been a long week. After arriving in Fort Bragg, we just got a bite to eat and got ready for slumber. Kayla rarely ate more than two meals a day, so I snacked between our breakfast and dinner.

On Saturday, June 16th, we visited the Mendocino Botanical Gardens and went to the farm on-site. One of the things I appreciate most about Kayla is that she is willing to try a new thing if it's safe. I appreciated eating farm-fresh strawberries right out of the field.

As we roamed the thirty-acre gardens, I walked along paths I had traveled before just to get Kayla's response to the vistas. After leaving the gardens, we got adventurous and took the Skunk Train. I was hoping the name of the train would not be reflected in any strange odors. It was a picturesque railroad journey through the woods. After we returned, we drove 20 miles to Leggett to drive through a tree. I loved driving through the Chandelier Tree, which predates Jesus. I had seen a picture of this tree at six years old while reading the World Book Encyclopedia and resolved one day to drive through it. As I passed through the tree, I noticed a poem etched in wood by Joseph B. Strauss called "The Redwoods." Here is an excerpt:

Here, sown by the Creator's hand,
In serried ranks, the Redwoods stand;
No other clime is honored so,
No other lands their glory know

The greater of Earth's living forms,
Tall conquerors that caught at storms;
Their challenge still unanswered rings,
Through fifty centuries of kings.

The nations that with them were young,
Rich empires, with their forts far-flung,
Lie buried now—their splendor gone;
But these proud monarchs still live on.

So shall they live when ends our day,
When our crude citadels decay;
For brief the years allotted man.
But infinite perennials span.

This is their temple, vaulted high,
And here we pause with reverent eye,
With silent tongue and awe-struck soul;
For, here we sense life's proper goal;

To be like these, straight, true, and fine,
To make our world, like theirs, a shrine;
Sink down, Oh, trap teller, on our knees,
God stands before you in these trees.

Motivated by the poem, I immediately gave my iPhone to Kayla, knelt on my knees, and gave homage to the Redwoods. These monumental groves have inspired me since I first saw them in 1968. It was a blessing to share the backstory so she could understand their impact on my life. We ended our weekend the next morning at a local breakfast nook in Fort Bragg and drove home, thankful for another father-daughter getaway. Kayla slept all the way home, and I felt blessed for this precious time together.

At the end of July, one of my lifelong desires came to completion. I had always wanted to go to every state in the republic, and Alaska was my fiftieth state. This journey began early in my teens when my father attended church conferences in various parts of the United States, followed by a vacation with the family. Twenty-two years in the military allowed me to almost complete the dream.

We were accompanied by Winsome and Rudy on this majestic adventure. The Alaskan cruise was better even than I had expected. Every time we stepped on deck, we viewed snow-covered mountains and glaciers descending into the sea.

On special excursions, we traveled on railroads up the White Pass and Yukon Route, where early explorers would spend all day going up and down the mountain in search of gold. During other stops, we cruised on the Auke Bay in search of whales. One day, I hope to return to Ketchikan, the salmon capital of the world, and bring home enough salmon to fill our freezer.

The unexpected blessing of this trip was the beauty of Vancouver. Between Grouse Point and Capilano River Regional Park, we were left in awe by more snow-capped mountains rising above the sea and walkways in the middle of the forest. This trip was a wonderland for adults; no theme parks were needed. Truly, we felt at one with nature.

Chapter Forty-Four

The John Muir Spirit

"I will lift up my eyes to the hills—From whence comes my help?"
Psalm 121:1

After returning from Vancouver, my heart was focused on the annual Great Reno Hot Air Balloon Race, the second weekend in September 2018. This is the world's largest free hot-air ballooning event. I started coming to this event in September 2013 and never missed even if I had to wake up at 3 a.m. and drive two hours to Reno from Sacramento.

I liked this festival because balloons, to me, represented prayers sent to God. My requests over the years have been answered or augmented by the grace of God. Through these supplications, I learned resilience, which renewed my confidence in God's will. At an early age, I prayed my life would have an impact. At every turn on the "highway of holiness," I desired personal, familial, and transformational changes. The balloons that floated upward at dawn symbolized morning prayers sent toward the throne of grace. The event was also personalized when a co-worker sang the National Anthem. This festival honored veterans, lifted military involvement, and supported families worldwide. Hospitality was the peculiar quality of these attendees.

As I walked the field to photograph the floating aerials, strangers stopped and asked, "Can you take a picture of me and my children, or me and my wife?"

I always said, "Sure."

Without hesitation, they returned the favor if I needed a picture taken.

Though the attendees were diverse, there was no sense of the divisiveness that so often characterizes public events. Everyone had come to share in the enjoyment. I wished this kind of camaraderie could be felt everywhere people gathered. This vibe of friendliness was similar to what it felt like in the sixties when people at gatherings shared music, art, or spirituality sincerely because they cared for one another.

This event also gave me an opportunity to play. Growing up in the South, I had to be serious around church folks, and the church was a pivotal point of our family life. After sitting behind the pulpit for perceived misbehavior, I did not want to be an embarrassment to my father. So, I tempered my adventurous spirit during childhood and adolescence because I feared my father's wrath.

Attendance at the balloon festival unleashed my playful side. Many of the balloons had cartoon characters that reminded me of my early years when I watched Tweety Bird on Saturday mornings. I loved laughing at them, but I'm glad my life was not a joke. The drama of these characters taught me valuable lessons about cats and mice, the dark saga of Darth Vader, and Wile E. Coyote, who utilized elaborate plans to catch his prey but failed every time. In a large way, the balloons reflected my life now.

This balloon event symbolized Act Three of my life. It represented philosophical victories. The balloons allowed me to review what had manifested in my life, what had expanded and taken flight. God gave me ministry opportunities to get myself off the ground, and His Holy Spirit lifted me and allowed me to speak the truth to the world.

The next event that inspired me was a visit to Yosemite National Park on May 31st, 2019. This had been a banner year for snow. In the fifty-one years of visiting this park, I had never seen the waterfalls inundate the surrounding areas. Bridal Veil Falls was so powerful that the runoff saturated the parking lot. As we walked along the paths near lower Yosemite Falls, the splash was so awesome we could not stand on the bridge for more than 30 seconds. The force from it felt like a 100 mph hurricane as the wind blew us from side to side.

We rode up to Glacier Point and looked at the snow-covered mountains. The peaks were covered with snow for a hundred miles, and the waterfalls splashed over the valley. It was a majestic sight. I was in photography heaven as we captured vistas from different angles.

This was, again, an appropriate occasion to reflect on my life experience. The familiar vistas of Yosemite prepared me for the mountaintop experiences of my life. The boulders filled me with memories of my father preaching at Glacier Point and his mischievous way of scaring us in the middle of the night with large bumble bee-shaped coat hangers. Dad taught us how to enjoy nature, with its highs and lows. Visiting Yosemite was an acknowledgment that these moments had paid off.

While hiking, I realized I had picked up the John Muir spirit of adventure and passion for exploration. I yearned to find out what was behind a tree, the origin of the river, and how the stream flowed. I'm glad I spent enough time in the wilderness to understand that this spirit would never leave me. I prayed that as I met others, they would catch that spirit and explore the sacred places and deeper crevices of their lives.

I had planned to retire on October 31st, 2019, and visit my daughter and grandchildren in November. I chose October 31st because I considered this date the worst day on the calendar. I never liked America's fascination with Halloween, haunted houses, and preoccupation with the dead. Having my retirement date on October 31st would change my perspective on the day. However, the retirement ceremony was postponed because of a glitch in the Human Resources department. I had to work an additional eight months, but it did not stop me from making my scheduled visit. I always desired to spend time with Alecia on her birthday, and this was the year to make that happen. In November 2019, that dream came to fruition. I flew to Dallas and spent time with Alecia (Lelee) for her birthday on November 8th and with my grandkids, Faith, Moriah, and DJ.

Fortunately, when I got to Alecia's home in McKinney, Texas, the grandchildren were available. I was glad I got to celebrate her birthday. I love birthdays, so I bought balloons, and the grandkids loved seeing them circulate on the ceiling between the vents.

On the first day, while the grandchildren were in school, I went to the Texas Discovery Gardens. They had a spectacular butterfly exhibit, where they let young butterflies fly away until they became comfortable with the process of moving their wings before being released into the enclosed garden. This was a caring environment for the butterflies to develop in. The atmosphere was symbolic of how God had placed me in anointed territories to learn the skills of ministry, preaching, teaching, and evangelism. That day, I visualized the largest butterfly or moth I had ever seen. The African moth is at least ten inches across.

I loved spending time with my daughters. Although I spent at least fifteen years with Alecia, our quality time had been aborted because of the separation and divorce from Angel. There were parts of my life that my daughters didn't know about and parts they didn't care to ask. But as we got older, we became more vulnerable and honest with each other and were able to look back and laugh.

I always wanted to be a father, and when I started dating Angel, Alecia was fifteen months old. It took a few months to take on fatherly responsibilities, but I never shied from those duties. When Angel and I got married, I adopted Alecia as my child, and she received all the rights of inheritance. Because Alecia had more actual time with me, she understood some of the trials and tribulations I endured to protect, feed, and care for the family. Having three children herself now, I believe Alecia understands daily the complexity of a parent's role.

From a biblical perspective, I was living the Christian understanding of adoption. As a Christian, I was adopted into the family of God when I received Christ as my Savior. I received Alecia and gave her everything I had to ensure her well-being. The Christian concept and the realities of adoption were made real to me through adopting Alecia. We took adoption to another level because Alecia and I have a wonderful rapport. It was the kind of rapport that I desired with all my daughters.

Being with the grandchildren this time was different from earlier visits. I got to see Faith play her bass clarinet. I saw Moriah's acting theatrics, and DJ exhibited all the boxing moves he had learned. Each child had acquired skills they were proud of. I especially enjoyed taking them to the mall to purchase some clothing items and joining them on the merry-go-round. We smiled and laughed as we bobbed on the horses. The times I had wished for with my own children, I finally got a chance to enjoy with grandchildren.

Chapter Forty-Five

The Hardest Thing I Ever Did

"And the Scripture was fulfilled, which says, 'Abraham be-lieved God...and he was called the friend of God.'"
James 2:23

After 6,000 deaths in China in December 2019, the World Health Organization declared a global health emergency. I was glad then that Human Resources had miscalculated my retirement. If there was ever a time when I needed to be in the epicenter of a health crisis, it was now. There were only two chaplains at our hospital, and I was glad to be part of the tag team with Chaplain Frank Yapp. Weekly, we had at least three briefings on COVID-19, and we took every precaution every day. At one point during the pandemic, we were averaging twenty-five COVID-19 cases per day for a sixty-two-bed hospital. It looked like a war zone.

Everyone was checked at the various entrances to the hospital. We had security all around the hospital in case someone tried to get in without answering the appropriate questions. People were lined up fifty deep for vaccines. They closed the auditorium and cafeteria and filled them with nurses to cope with the onslaught of individuals receiving vaccines. On the third floor, some rooms were converted into COVID-19 wards to handle the wave of patients. I carried latex gloves in my pocket and had to learn not to shake hands. I fist-bumped or elbowed the staff. The chaplain staff moved from in-person assessments to Zoom calls because of the health risk of direct contact. Because of my comorbidities, I would see only the non-COVID-19 patients: Chaplain Yapp saw those who were COVID-19 carriers. I maintained a protocol for ensuring a high level of immunity. I drank alkaline water, ate an alkaline diet, and maintained physical activity and a good sleep pattern. When my wife got COVID-19, I knew what I needed to do to quarantine myself.

The most difficult part of dealing with COVID-19 was that no family members were allowed in the hospital. As chaplains, we became the surrogate family for the patients. The staff who experienced the highest degree of burnout worked in the Emergency Department (ER). Unfortunately, ER was one area that was most highly contagious. When patients came to the ER, we often could not interview them. When we did, they would say there was someone in their family with COVID-19. During this period, at least three of the nurses that I had known since 2016 left the hospital and moved to another facility. We were losing many staff because of transfers, so the hospital paid us extra to stay. Three staff I had worked with at VA Reno died from COVID-19 during the first month of the pandemic. One of them was a lab technician who came into my office twice a week. He told me his dream job was being a chaplain. I loved the work, but at this point, there were only two of us providing critical support for thirteen hospitals. Throughout the entire pandemic, we monitored deaths across the nation, particularly in counties surrounding Sacramento.

Throughout the health crisis, I felt a heightened appreciation from hospital administration, staff, and patients. Usually, the chaplain is rarely called upon unless there is a crisis. We are rarely contacted to assist with the daily organizational planning. With this health scare, the organization realized staff and patients fare better when chaplains are involved. For once in my institutional career, COVID-19 placed chaplains at the center of the planning discussion. We were considered critical staff. Illness for the patients and the staff was inevitable. Our role as caregivers and surrogate family members became crucial. We were called into family meetings on a regular basis to bring a pastoral approach and empathetic perspective to dire situations.

Then, another crisis happened. After George Floyd was murdered by a police officer in Minneapolis, Minnesota, on May 25th, 2020, the racial temperature rose in America. Our executive administrators sent chaplains to the thirteen clinics to assess how staff was dealing with COVID-19 but also with racial tension in the clinics. As we visited each clinic, we talked with site managers and staff. It was the most challenging task I had been called to perform, but I felt honored to be entrusted with assessing the medical/racial climate of each clinic with a written report.

As I prepared again to retire at the end of June 2020, a part of me was wrestling with the idea of retirement. I knew I needed to move on to the next stage in my life, but I didn't know what that would look like. I had considered some community college courses, but when I researched those options, no one was conducting in-person classes. As a life-long learner, I wanted to keep my mind active. The word "retirement" had its own challenge. For me, it denoted leaving one's career or withdrawing from service. I have been involved in ministry for forty years and have seen nothing in the Bible about retirement. The question was how could I continue to be involved in ministry.

As I pondered retirement, I asked, "How could I continue to be involved in ministry?" Part of my answer came through a poetry class. My first desire was to find a class on Black Literature. As I searched, I found that most of the classes available were in another part of the nation where I probably would never meet the professor. Fortunately, I saw an advertisement for the

Community Literature Initiative in Los Angeles. After filling out an application, I had to be interviewed. To my surprise, I was interviewed by someone else. I thought that was strange, but I flowed with the process. I was elated when they sent an email saying I was accepted into the program. That gave me incredible satisfaction after my four-month search.

As the holidays approached, we decided to host my Birthday Gala again on the first Saturday of December, on my birthday, December 4th. The birthday preparations were an easy way to motivate Susan to get the house together for Christmas. She loved the extra incentive. Susan hired a disc jockey, Michael, whose musical selections almost caused me to get my saxophone and play along. As the party approached for the time to sing "Happy Birthday" and cut the cake, I took the liberty to recite one of my poems, entitled "With a Christmas Heart."

The prophet Isaiah prophesied seven centuries ago,
About a Messiah who will bring a divine glow,
A great light for the world, for everyone to see,
A light to live in you, a candle to glow in me;

With this light burning bright in our life,
It brings harmony and peace to minimize strife;
No doubt God is with us, Immanuel is made plain,
Hope is restored, which allows us to sustain;

Once again, we gather as family and friends,
To renew hope in each other with ways to transcend;
Never forget the wonder of this season, how God sent His Son,
To give a plan of eternal redemption for everyone;

Let's take a moment, pause and reflect,
And find ways to exhibit our heart-inspired intellect;
Appreciate your brother and sister with eyes of glee,

Find non-judgmental ways we can all agree;

Forgiveness is available in small bites or big,
Utilize the paradigm of Christ that will never renege;
When we do, we may once again reveal,
The supernatural power and miracle of love to heal.

As a result of the COVID-19 pandemic, we thought the best way to spend the holidays in 2020 was to check on one of my daughters. Because of the high level of stress in Los Angeles, Naivasha decided to move to Oahu, Hawaii, in the fall of 2020. Her two options were Mexico or Hawaii. It was a great time to get away from California because of the cold, and there were very few individuals going to Hawaii. Naivasha was in transition, moving from one apartment to another. Her new location had room to keep her hibiscus plants. She could practice her photography and enjoy the great vistas of Oahu.

For me, any time with Vasha was quality time. Over the past ten years, Vasha has had business ventures in Los Angeles and New York. I thought this move would help her with self-care. I had spent almost half of my Reserve duty in Hawaii and felt comfortable in the laid-back culture. I appreciated Vasha's advice about eating locations when we got there and enjoyed spending time both at her older apartment and at the new one. I'm glad, as a parent, I was able to help Vasha out with the purchase of beds and other furnishings. Though she was two thousand miles away, she seemed happier. Hawaii was part of her dream to one day have some property and expand her hibiscus-growing enterprise. I continue to encourage Naivasha's dreams and send her love by text or phone call.

Entering the New Year, the theme of Kwanza 365 kept revolving in my head. I had become so enamored with the thought of familiarizing the public with Black history and culture that I created a black invention calendar for 2021 entitled

"Giants of Invention, Scientists of Discovery." I once again embraced an Afro-centric way of thinking.

In the middle of summer 2021, a pastor friend named De-Wayne passed away unexpectedly in the Dallas area. He was a cousin to my former wife, Angel, but I felt that I needed to go to the funeral and support the family. I had been married to Angel for sixteen years, and though we were no longer together, we were both committed to supporting our children. Both of Angel's two brothers still treated me like their brother, which made me feel like part of the family. The dissolution of marriage did not dissolve the heartfelt bond between brothers in Christ. Because I had been removed from the family connections, I had to explain myself during my four-day stay when people asked me, "Who are you?"

I felt uncomfortable saying, "I am Angel's former husband," but that was the only way some of the senior aunts and uncles recognized me. I believe my presence brought comfort to the family. Moreover, because I brought my camera, I was able to take several pictures of the eight siblings. I was also introduced to Louis, Alecia's new friend, who had helped her through challenging times in her life. I felt comfortable that I could call Louis anytime to ensure Alecia was alright.

Amid my poetry reflections, one of my best friends died, Byron Clayton Thompson. I had known Byron since our sophomore year in high school. "King," as we called each other, was my only Black roommate in college at UC Davis. He graduated from law school and set up a law practice in downtown Oakland. As a man of distinction, he threw me a bachelor party in January 1984 before I married Angel. Unfortunately, Byron was involved in a car accident in 2005. He had been convalescing in a hospital or skilled nursing facility since then. As a CPE intern, I was glad he was on my caseload at Herrick Hospital in Berkeley. I would prayerfully sit by his bed and ponder life.

Chapter Forty-Six

Latter Years Better Than the Former

"For whatever is born of God overcomes the world. And this is the victory that has overcome the world—our faith."
1 John 5:4

With Byron's passing, several thoughts came to mind. The Bible says that our latter years will be better than our former years. In my case, this has been absolutely true. My former years were rough; I was born in segregation and weaned in climates of explicit and implicit bias. I could not speak to my parents freely or with the opposite sex because of fear. These, as well as an actual speech impediment, meant I had no voice in my early years. Now, with the gift of poetry, prose, and preaching, I could speak my mind freely.

I believe God brought me through seasons of crucible because of humility, so this poem, "Humble Yourself," is dedicated to my life journey.

Humble yourself
to the crystal bead
of perfect humility,
No matter how holy
you advance,
One can never
be free of

blind spots.

Humble yourself
prostrate your heart
to the blade of grass,
See ego shrivel
in the ground crust
of dry-burnt moss,
and you will find
the seed.

Humble yourself
to the stream
that flows
to the ocean,
Lay flat
and you will
find humility that
gives the
ocean power.

Humble yourself
Press in naked
without old garments,
be useful
show your
vulnerability.

Humble yourself
to the way of the leper,
be human, like Naaman
go wash seven times
in the dirty Jordan River.

At the moment of openness, remove all debris,
let this virtue shine
in the pearl of true humility!

September 2021 rolled around, and the Community Literature Initiative presented another poetry class offering. I joined
this alumni class because my poetry book was still in process,
and I wanted to finish it. The class gave me the opportunity to
improve my craft and add more poems to the book. I had several ideas about publication, but the World Stage Press offered
the best opportunity for publication. Reading and working on a
poem was challenging because, at times, I didn't feel I was doing my best work, but the teachers encouraged me. The more I
wrote, the more revelation came in my direction.

I began to spend at least one day a week at the African Mar-
ket in Sacramento. I attended the Black History program at Sacramento State University and spoke to vendors about my upcoming book. The book editing and review process was more
time-consuming than anticipated. It took thirteen revisions,
back and forth with my editors, from January to early April, but
I was determined to meet the April deadline.

Finally, I got the confirmation that April 22nd, Earth Day
2022, was going to be my book release. I asked my older sister
Ronita to sing "The Impossible Dream." I asked a friend I had
known since seminary, Don Matthews, to speak words of affirmation, and I asked one of my fellow poets, Greta, to recite one
of her transformative poems. The event was hosted by Camari
Carter Hawkins, who was the teacher for my inaugural class.
Her encouragement had gotten me through the challenges and
difficulties of writing and speaking my poetry.

Thanking God for an opportunity to stay mentally active, I
applied to go back and work with the Department of Veteran
Affairs for three days a week. The previous supervisor, who had
given me a headache and caused my blood pressure to rise, had

left. I went back mostly to help Chaplain Yapp with the work-load. I knew the demands were too great for one chaplain, es-pecially with COVID-19 continuing and increased on-call re-sponsibilities. So, I was accepted to work on an hourly status for three days, which I reduced to two days when I was needed to help with the caretaking responsibilities of my 99-year-old mother. I worked Mondays and Wednesdays, which lightened Chaplain Yapp's workload and allowed him to leave on time. Working part-time helped me deal with the lingering discom-forts related to retirement.

Having poetry as a possible avocation helped me finally de-cide to resign permanently from the hospital. Hospitalizations of COVID-19 patients had gone down, and new management was in the process of hiring another chaplain. It was time to move on. I had worked my eight-plus years and more, and com-ing back as a Fee-Basis helped me emotionally and spiritually to come to terms gradually with my feelings about retirement. When I left this time, I did not look back; it was time to make the transition.

Several staff asked me for advice about retiring. Word had gotten around that my retirement had been postponed and be-came unusually complicated. I felt like I was back in the Navy giving advice to sailors.

They approached me, curious. "Thomas, I heard you had problems when you wanted to retire."

"Yes, I went to Human Resources and found out two days before my scheduled retirement that they had miscalculated the date by eight months."

"That must have been a shock!"

"Yes, it was, but in a positive way. I was able to be here for the pandemic. I would have hated having to leave the VA when the hospital was in a time of critical need."

The staff understood that my situation was unique. COVID-19 answered my desire to be needed because I really was needed. I had never felt so integral to the lives of staff and patients as I was during the pandemic. I do not wish for another pandemic, but I'm glad for the way it gave new meaning to the term chaplaincy. The importance of chaplains' roles became clearer in those months.

As I turned my attention to the poetry course, I reflected that God had sent me this desire to explore poetry as a sign and revelation of my calling after so-called "retirement." In response to one of my memoir assignments, I penned this prose, "Why I Write."

> I write for the ancestors, who never had the opportunity to learn an alphabet or write or form a sentence because it was against the law to learn.
> I write for those who were whipped, maimed, and hanged for writing.
> I write for ancestors who had the words printed on their birth certificate indicating that their parents "Cannot read or write."
> I write for all the children I taught in Africa who had no food or water to nourish their brains, for those who woke up with no pencils or pens or pads of paper where they could articulate the emotions of their hearts.
> I write for all the people who have a spiritual injury.
> I write for all the parishioners who have been hurt in the name of religion.
> I write for all the inmates, soldiers, and patients who have been institutionalized but never received healing or recovery.
> I write for traumatized people who are still waiting for someone to listen to their pain.
> I write for the individuals who have experienced PTSD in war, both the soldiers and the innocent bystanders.

I write for the underdogs, for the people who were told they would "never be nothing" because they came from parents who were nothing and a generation of people who were nothing.

I write for biblical persons like Job—persecuted, bewildered, tried in ways beyond understanding.

I write for the people in the world who are misunderstood by their brethren, with no clue of God's mercy.

I write for the Josephs in the world who have been thrown into slavery and ended up in prison, waiting for a blessing to lift them from their plight.

I write because the spirit of Frederick Douglass is upon me. The same fight Douglass engaged in continues.

I write because the spirit of the Harlem Renaissance hovers over me.

I write for the watchmen in the night who must proclaim the revelation that they receive, or blood will be on their hands.

Made in the USA
Middletown, DE
11 July 2024